To [illegible] very

good friend, This

Book is about all the

Problems of human beings

which we hope the eternal

intelligence of univers

will solve for ever.

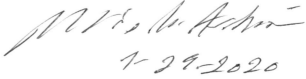

1-29-2020

The Echo of Eternal Awareness

Misha Ashoorian and Marilyn Priel

The Echo of Eternal Awareness
Misha Ashoorian and Marilyn Priel

Published by:
ROSSWOOD PUBLISHING
2037 Rosswood Dr.
San Jose, CA 95124, U.S.A.

ISBN 978-0-9797519-0-5

Book Design and cover watercolour painting by
www.KareenRoss.com

Dedication

To all who wonder.

Preface

This book began as an interview for a television program. I was going to ask Misha Ashoorian about his illustrious career as an actor and writer. I also planned a separate interview about ancient Assyria, the land of his people in what is now Iraq. In conversations we began having, I discovered there was something of paramount importance in his life, far more meaningful to him than all the celebrity he had experienced. Mr. Ashoorian had wondered as a small boy why many of his dreams came true. He began a lifelong study of things spiritual and metaphysical, attending numerous classes in Iran and the United States, studying with dervishes, and reading hundreds of books on all related subjects.

I was astounded at the scope of information he had gleaned and held in his memory almost like an encyclopedia. I thought he might share some of it with people who have a curiosity, but not the time and years to pursue such studies. Almost every world leader throughout history has been influenced by metaphysics or spirituality.

For a very long time he was reluctant to do a book, fearing people would think he was attempting to teach or impose certain ideas. I convinced him that if he just honestly summarized some of the things he has learned, it might result in more fair and interesting descriptions than those of writers proving a point. What began as questions and answers, became more of a conversation, and as we talked, opinions did, at times, form in our minds.

We hope you will read with interest and curiosity, and form your own opinions. But, to read Mr. Ashoorian's descriptions in the words of a poet, you will be fascinated.

Marilyn Priel

Introduction

Priel:

Mr. Ashoorian, thank you for agreeing to talk with me.

Ashoorian:

I do admit, Ms. Priel, that you had to work long and hard to convince me to do so. However, when I learned through our discussions that you are a person of integrity, I began looking forward with interest to telling you about whatever you might ask.

Priel:

Your parents are of the ancient Assyrian nation in Mesopotamia, which had an empire reaching far beyond the Middle East in the seventh century B.C. After World War I, it became Iraq. Ethnic Assyrians still live there in the northern part near the ancient capital of Nineveh. Your mother's family had remained in the same villages for thousands of years, despite the invasions and occupations of many later empires. When she was thirteen, her parents and other villagers were killed in a massacre, and she fled on foot into Russia. Later she met and married your father, and they soon returned to the little villages of her people which have inspired so much of your poetry. Not long after, they decided their Christian beliefs would be better tolerated in Iran, and that became your home for more than forty years.

Ashoorian:

My fondest recollections of my youth are of my visits to my cousins at those farms and Assyrian villages. We ran barefoot, and caught fish with our hands. Everyone worked, and sang, and ate, and loved. And, yes, I grew up in Iran, in the modern capital of Tehran. We had a relatively nice life there. We had our own neighborhoods of Assyrians, our own private schools, and the Shah's regime was tolerant of religious observances. He was progressive, and the nation and my family became prosperous.

Priel:

You became famous as an actor and writer when you were quite young. In fact, you were the leading man…a matinee idol…on stage and in motion pictures, enjoying that exciting and creative environment.

Ashoorian:

I consider myself lucky that by my early twenties I was a professional in the company of the best theatre in Tehran. The Shah and Queen Farrah were promoting culture. We were treated with utmost respect, and were encouraged in our pursuits. Lots of money was flowing everywhere, so we and the arts were flourishing. The pleasure I enjoyed in those days is undeniable.

Priel:

Aside from all of your star image, you are most revered among your Assyrian people for your lyrics. When did you begin the writing phase of your career?

Ashoorian:

I was writing poetry and lyrics when I was a teenager. I had the amazing good fortune to collaborate with the most talented composers and musicians of my nation, continuing until today. I was a playwright, and one of the Ministry of Culture and Arts certified authors for cinema and television. But, as you mentioned, the writings my people enjoy the most are my poetry and lyrics. There are over three hundred, actually, about our Assyrian history, village life, and love, many of which have been set to music. I cannot even express to you how much I love my Assyrian heritage.

Priel:

The tremendous devotion you have for your Assyrian heritage is evidenced by the fact that throughout your adult life you have been continuously active in maintaining the culture and welfare of the people. How, then, did you become so heavily immersed in spiritual subjects?

Ashoorian:

That was something which was a part of me like my skin. When I was a small child, I had dreams which would come true. I also had premonitions which came true. It led to my lifelong search to understand how those things could be happening. I began in my early twenties studying with Sufis in Iran. It really has been my passion taking classes, reading, and learning all my life everything I could about things spiritual.

Priel:

I'm intrigued, and eager to begin hearing some of the information you've acquired.

Ashoorian:

It will be my pleasure.

Priel:

Let us begin, then, with what most people believe is the beginning of everything, and lighter subjects can follow soon after.

Contents

Consciousness

and

Intelligence

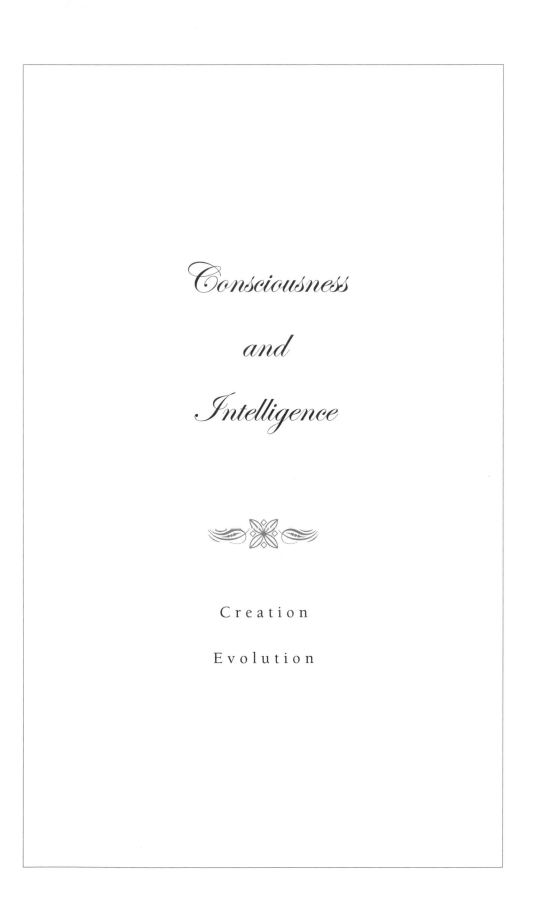

Creation

Evolution

~ C r e a t i o n ~

Priel:

People from the beginning of mankind, and at all parts of the earth, have believed in a supreme power to bestow good and bad upon them. One might wonder if there is something in DNA which causes us to have that concept, the same as it's in people's genes to create, and to have curiosity. We all know that from the very beginnings of history humans have had different images about a creator and the emanation of the entire universe. What could really be the cause of it?

Ashoorian:

The cause of it is cosmic motion, eternal and ceaseless, like a living fire. As has been said from ancient times, a universal soul is the cause of every phenomenon in nature.

Priel:

Is that the same as the God concept in world religions?

Ashoorian:

Yes, whatever term is used, it is God, a cosmic soul, or a pure, formless and unknown essence of absolute intelligence. According to esoteric doctrine teachings like Buddhism, and Brahmanism of the Hindus, one infinite and unknown essence existed from all eternity with no beginning and no end. They call it the day and night of Brahma. An out breathing of that unknown essence produces the universe, and inhalation causes it to disappear. Of course, this is allegorical, possibly to the Big Bang and its collapse—an expanding and cooling. They believe this process has been going on from all eternity, and that our present universe is only one of an infinite series. Well, scientists now consider that possibility.

The Secret Doctrine, by Madame Helena Blavatsky, the famous Russian founder of Theosophy, tells that the real cause of our universe cannot be given, because even the highest masters have never been able to penetrate those boundaries of knowledge.

Priel:

Some scholars call it divine thought. Some, universal consciousness or universal mind. What do you say about that?

Ashoorian:

Buddhism calls it universal consciousness, or universal awareness. However, when we say thought, there is a question mark. It has been said that thoughts are a product of intelligence and awareness in the universe and the human kingdom. This is a fundamental reality. Our awareness and consciousness work through the brain and produce thoughts. But they don't require a brain to exist. Awareness and consciousness exist without the existence of brain and thought.

Priel:

The question of all questions, was there a purpose for the creation? Is there a purpose for the universe? If all ideas were combined, is there at least some general consistency which would enable one to determine a reason?

Ashoorian:

The purpose for the magnificent conducting of this fascinating orchestration is beyond the power of human comprehension. According to various philosophies of ancient times, a super divine awareness existed prior to the beginning of the physical universe, before time and space, in the deep silence of the void. It was a kind of formless intelligence which had the pattern of all the forms of creation in mind. For some reason beyond human perception this super divine awareness held a great urge for manifestation in a physical level. There was a desire to create matter from plasma in the deep void of space.

Priel:

Do you mean the Big Bang theory, or Quantum Physics, or some other theories?

Ashoorian:

The Big Bang theory, as I talked about earlier, was a process which has been going on from all eternity, and our present universe is one of countless previous Big Bangs. However, the theory of Quantum Physics can be described differently. The great desire I mentioned before can be considered a virtual idea that is a pure idea in the mind of cosmic soul. The moment that idea and great desire touched the mind of the universal intelligence, the process of creation took place toward formation of our physical universe. When this was completed, quantum physics was accomplished. It means quantum physics was completed in three stages. The first one is the idea, the second is the process of the idea which can be called quantum, and the third is the completion of the physical universe. This theory is Quantum Physics. This might be close to what happened.

Priel:

Scientists have declared that life came into existence by chance. For example, there is the notion that if the distance between Earth and its sun were a little bit off, we would not have had life on our planet. If that is so, what would be the role of a creator?

Ashoorian:

The notion of accident, or chance, might have been exactly in the thought of the creator, or cosmic designer, prior to time and space. By chance, or otherwise, doesn't matter. What matters is the combination of essential matter which contained the potentiality to cause our physical universe and the life we have today. There are two or three hundred billion stars in our Milky Way galaxy. If any of those stars is in the right location, and has a planet in the right position and distance to it, life can begin. That is because there is an order, or code, in the entire universe. Either phenomenon, chance or the will of the creator to make obedience to the order, would result in manifestation of life. Why? Because all those billions of stars have almost the same portions of material and gases as our sun, which are 75% Hydrogen, 20% Helium, and 5% other types of gases.

Priel:

In any case, the cause precedes the effect.

Ashoorian:

When we look at the tapestry of the structure of our world, and the pattern and formation of the law of physics, it does seem natural that this masterpiece could be by purpose and design. To further that idea is a quotation from Paul Davies, in his book, ***God and the New Physics.***

"That the universe is ordered seems self-evident. Everywhere we look, from the far-flung galaxies to the deepest recesses of the atom, we encounter regularity with intricate organization. We do not observe matter or energy to be distributed chaotically. They are arranged, instead, in a hierarchy of structure, and so on. Moreover, the behavior of physical systems is not haphazard, but lawful and systematic. Scientists frequently experience a sense of awe and wonder at the subtle beauty and elegance of nature."

Albert Einstein said, "God doesn't play dice." I'll never forget something I read many years ago in one of the important scientific magazines. The world's greatest scientists had been working to discover the cause of creation. They concluded all their findings at a large conference, and declared, whatever there is, God's fingertip is in it.

~E v o l u t i o n~

Priel:

So the physical universe is created, and all animals and plants, no matter how primitive their structure and development, function uniformly and efficiently. How could they have evolved according to their needs?

Ashoorian:

It was intrinsic in all aspects of nature, by the guidance of universal intelligence. Probably, we have to go back as far as the time that cells began their formation. Since then, every pattern and form on our planet began their effort for self formation just to follow the design and model that has been placed for them by the first order of universal intelligence.

The process of human beings has had the highest perfect form on our planet. We have a kind of absolute totality that is due to our awakened condition in life. All those processes toward completion are a kind of obedience of our first atom and molecular structure code given toward evolution.

Priel:

What kind of code might that be?

Ashoorian:

It was believed by many ancient sages that there are an infinite number of invisible form fields which design and determine the shape of all the creatures, animals, plants, and human beings. For example, when one organism succeeds in creating a certain shape, immediately it is setting up a kind of invisible pattern or a resonance in motion which will affect any other organism in the same frequency.

When the process of evolution started, the first archetypes came into existence. Archetypes are the first structures in nature from which all patterns and designs in the physical world were copied and brought forth. Since then, the memory became inherent, and each cell retained the first order in its subconscious.

For instance, if we take a watermelon seed and keep it ten years, twenty years, or more, then take the seed to our backyard and put it in the soft soil and water it, after a while we will see exactly the same watermelon we ate so long ago. The memory of that seed is eternal. That is how archetype has been processing since the beginning. This is the code of the universal order which must be obeyed. We have to keep in mind that memory is inherent in the entire universe.

Priel:
Where are these memories stored, and how are living things having access to these kinds of memories?

Ashoorian:
Possibly, from collective unconscious, as Carl Jung, the psychoanalyst, suggests. Or, from the mind of our invisible architect. Look at a snowflake, or frost on a window in winter time. See the magnificence of their pattern. Look at the beauty of a tiger, a bird in flight, or human beings. How perfect they have been designed.

Priel:
Isn't that evolution? We've been told that necessity is the cause of evolution. So evolution has shaped and designed them.

Ashoorian:

Of course, it is evolution, but evolution needs to have awareness, or intelligence, to feel the necessity of evolving. It needs a guidance to evolve. How can matter evolve without awareness. We have to keep in mind that beyond this mysterious phenomenon there is only one source, and that is God, or cosmic soul, like an echo of a current stream of intelligence passing through the vein of all living creatures designing them the way they are. This is the ultimate truth.

Priel:

When you tell about this knowledge being beyond our power of comprehension, or perception, do you mean that our brains are not yet developed enough to understand? Or is it that mankind has not yet gathered enough knowledge to be able to understand?

Ashoorian:

It is believed that our brains and minds have not yet been developed to the essential level which allows us to interact beyond those mysterious boundaries. Man will eventually progress to function in a higher consciousness through a completely different dimension. It will be of a higher ethereal level.

That will be extraordinary for mankind. Human beings will interact through a superconscious state in a spiritual realm. Then, through spiritual ability he will tune in to that world of plan and pattern, and of past, present and future. When mankind can successfully interact through his superconsciousness by concentration and meditation, he will begin to obtain first hand information in a realm not related to words and time. He can learn and get all desired information instantaneously upon any subject. It means that all we have learned from the past is no longer necessary. Instead, mental preparation will take the place of memory. Eventually, knowledge through concentration and meditation will be a universal golden rule and the method for mankind.

Through its powers of meditation mankind will interact in this level where the world of actual plan and pattern of evolution will be revealed. It will learn the secret of the invisible architect. It is just beginning to happen since the start of the twentieth century. Vera Stanley Adler, has explained this phenomenon so well in her fascinating book, *The Fifth Dimension*.

Priel:

We know living things mutate in their evolving just a miniscule few at a time in a species until eventually all have evolved to the same level. One might suppose that the extrasensory abilities some few people possess in this current level are destined to become inherent in all mankind in further development. And, possibly what is considered a genius today will become typical intelligence eventually.

But, let's go back to that point where we talked about a universal intelligence flowing through all that there is—that God soul which puts the idea of function and evolution into all elements of life.

Ashoorian:

Universal intelligence, collective unconscious, or spirit guidance, all are related to one source which is God, or as the masters of antiquity put it, the "container" of all that exists. It has provided orders in the physical world and in the invisible world. If we raise our frequency to a higher level of spirituality and tap those superior energies, we will be aligned with universal law and order. In that state we are detached and liberated from the material world and become one with the eternal cosmic soul, or God.

Priel:

As part of the energy field, are there other things surrounding us which we don't see and don't comprehend? Is that part of the invisible thought fields you mentioned?

Ashoorian:

They say there are many other things in the invisible plane which we don't see. Probably, we only think they are invisible. It might really be due to the high speed of their activities, which could be beyond the ability of human sight to catch up to their speed of motion.

Priel:

I see what you mean. There is energy in the universe which we know is there, but can't see, like the various rays, for instance.

Ashoorian:

I was attending a class one time, and a student asked the instructor, "What is the meaning of metaphysical?" "Meta, is a Greek word meaning 'beyond'," the instructor explained. Then he lit a candle. "What do you see?", he asked the class. The answer was that they saw a candle, and a flame. "What else do you see?" he asked. No one answered. Then he put his hand over the flame. "If you come here," he said, " and put your hand three or four inches above the flame, you will feel heat. I can't see it, but still there is something here. That we cannot see it, doesn't mean that it doesn't exist."

Priel:

That is really a marvelous example. What about unseen entities?

Ashoorian:

Universal intelligence provides us with all information from collective unconscious. It's said that we receive guidance from spirits or other entities. It is said that there are invisible prespirits of deceased people, different entities both good and bad, that there are elemental spirits and the spirits of great masters, and a kind of beings which we call angels. In addition, there are other thought forms in motion which are indefinable. They say all these will be visible to us when we start interacting in the fifth dimension.

There will be a lot of changes in human life. We will be in a great process of transformation and transfiguration. All the invisible energies of spirit and elements will be revealed to us through our ethereal plane of that dimension. We just have to align our frequency to that magnificent, mysterious dimension.

Priel:

It seems like there wouldn't be much remaining to evolve to after that. What is said about anything beyond that?

Ashoorian:

Based upon my studies, mankind will ultimately comprehend the true nature and purpose of the physical universe, and will be able to turn toward his eternal divinity, the essence of God. However, I am not emphasizing a definite number of levels. There might be multi dimensions beyond.

Priel:

I'm actually confused about levels, or numbered dimensions. Since evolution progresses a small step at a time, how can it be sectioned off into numbered levels?

Ashoorian:

Numbered dimensions is a way of expressing levels we have reached which are a drastic and important improvement. I should go back to the time that mankind, after behaving and moving like animals, suddenly started behaving differently and raised onto two feet to walk erect. This was the greatest adventure of his life! What happened was not an ordinary process of evolution. In fact, it was really an incredible 'jump in evolution'! It seems that essential elements were created in his brain and mind which caused this jump in evolution. Probably, this was the start of our current level or dimension which began at that critical time.

Priel:

Was it a plan of nature that when humans became more aware they reached upright into the source of energy and enlightenment? Did they stand erect because they were instinctively moving and looking upwards for cosmic knowledge?

Ashoorian:

That is what I mean. In my opinion, at that critical time something happened! It might have been a plan in the mind of universal architect, or a source of divine awareness, which made man conscious to reach upright into the source of cosmic energy and look upward for knowledge. I believe some kind of elements were created in his system which caused this type of change and transformation in his life. Don't you think this was a kind of 'jump in evolution'?

Priel:

It might be, but there might be some other factors for our evolution which have not been clarified. From all that we have seen, humanity has had a gradual progression during thousands of years of history.

Ashoorian:

True. After that jump, mankind gradually was just functioning in the current dimension. He started making primitive tools and weapons, then gradually as civilization developed he made more sophisticated tools and weapons and invented the wheel and a form of writing. Although he later developed amazing skills in engineering, construction, and some of the sciences, this was the picture of our species until almost the end of the nineteenth century. At that time, a superbly higher technology appeared.

Priel:

What about the level even further advanced than now which you mentioned previously as having beginnings around the start of the twentieth century? Why should such be the case?

Ashoorian:

I am sure you have heard this expression, "Evolution is better than revolution." I personally agree with this expression. However, in the fifth level, evolution started accelerating so rapidly that the above mentioned expression does not apply to it. For a few minutes, let's imagine ourselves back at the end of the nineteenth century and visualize the progress humanity has achieved. We can see that after thousands of years, suddenly he began inventing incredible things. Electricity, the telephone, radio, automobiles, airplanes, television, engines for factories, and motors for appliances. Then came the computer, outer space capabilities, amazing communication devices, and wonderful medical cures and preventions. These brought us to the highest level of technology of all time, in a mere instant on earth.

In fact, those inventions, especially the computer and all the aspects related to it, would have seemed like the invisible world of magic in a box, beyond the power of comprehension in the eighteenth and nineteenth centuries. It is obvious that the level of evolution we have reached today is incomparable with all the past history of mankind. With all this in mind, don't you think this is much more than even a jump in evolution? In fact, I would say, it is a 'Revolution in Evolution'.

Priel:

Regarding the interaction of mankind in the ethereal plane in the next dimension, is this considered the cause of this rapid acceleration in our evolution?

Ashoorian:

We have to remember that the universe is continuously perfecting itself. That is the nature of the universe, and human beings as well.

Priel:

Is there more to come?

Ashoorian:

I will say, yes. It will be beyond our human's imagination.

Priel:

Atoms, and cells, and DNA and life. On and on. Cycling and recycling. Beyond humans developing, where and when did anything resembling people with some ability to create and express themselves in an abstract manner first surface?

Ashoorian:

Recently, DNA from an early African woman's remains has been traced through people across Asia, the Middle East and Europe. DNA from Semitic people has appeared to a small degree in prehistoric North and South America, and in the Gobi Desert. Inscriptions in caves all over the world have been found. Ancient legends tell of people tens of thousands of years ago. Some are quite similar, yet are from far distant lands.

Priel:

What is confusing to many people is that, when we follow biblical genealogy backwards, it appears that Adam and Eve were created only 7,000 years ago.

Ashoorian:

That has been the greatest argued subject between scientists and churches. In fact, it has puzzled me how Adam and Eve can be justified, when we see that scientists have dated those magnificent paintings on cave walls in France and Spain to be from almost 40,000 years ago. I think the churchmen should come up with strong evidence and solve this problem forever.

Priel:

The Neanderthals arrived and left. The ancient Sumerians wrote of people much older than themselves. Civilizations, like everything in the universe, seem to pulsate, in and out, dying and being reborn. Mud bricks crumble, stone structures get covered with dust, vegetation, water, and lava. There are visible pyramids everywhere—Southeast Asia, Mesopotamia, Egypt, South and Central America, North America has thousands, and more than a hundred are in the Gobi Desert area. How many prior civilizations thrived beneath those?

Ashoorian:

Tantalizing bits of archaeological information are being found which give a small inkling that ancient legends from many sources regarding older civilizations could be true. One of the most fascinating books one could read on the subject is Zecharia Sitchin's, *The 12th Planet*. Artifacts have been found depicting people wearing flying apparatus. It's not ridiculous to think that if we could invent a flying machine, another civilization could do it also with a different source of energy. Atlantis was said to have used the great power of crystal. Physics is physics, always and forever.

Priel:

On my mind is that rapid escalation of technology at the beginning of the twentieth century. What if there were other civilizations which had advanced technology, but had no written language, or perhaps a language which was undiscovered or was destroyed? After all, intelligent Cro-Magnons have been around for many thousands of years.

Albert Einstein, 26 years old in 1905, a mere patent clerk with a wife and child, envisioned and proved theories of the physical universe that changed our lives and the understanding of the universe. Miners in California, village shoemakers in Burgundy, Tibetan herders, natives in the Congo, most who couldn't read, and even educated bankers in

London as well, had no inkling or thought of such stupendous subjects. But Einstein did. One man. One genius. He alone. It would have taken only one genius in prehistory to envision theories and alter the lives of his civilization, for instance how to construct a great pyramid, a vehicle, or a concept of a written language.

Ashoorian:

It is interesting to think about. In the Smithsonian Magazine issue of April, 2005, there is an article about the existing tribe of Korubo in the Amazon. Naked with painted bodies, living in straw shelters with no knowledge of modern amenities, they are ignorant of any existence of the rest of the world. In the same issue, is an article about Dr. Jonas Salk, who in 1955 changed the world when he presented a vaccine he had conceived and developed to prevent crippling polio. Humans, living in the same century.

Ms. Priel, certainly extraordinary and recent archeological discoveries have altered opinions held for many years. And it is fascinating. But however many civilizations might have come and gone, and regardless of who came first or how similar they might be, basically, mankind has followed the ultimate path of an unstoppable progression in evolution and higher levels of mind elevation.

In the human kingdom, progress and development were due to our spiritual essence with cosmic soul, having a kind of totality related to universal intelligence. For this very reason, mankind has been considered the brilliant jewel of creation. This enabled us to become like co-creators in a very high level.

Beliefs

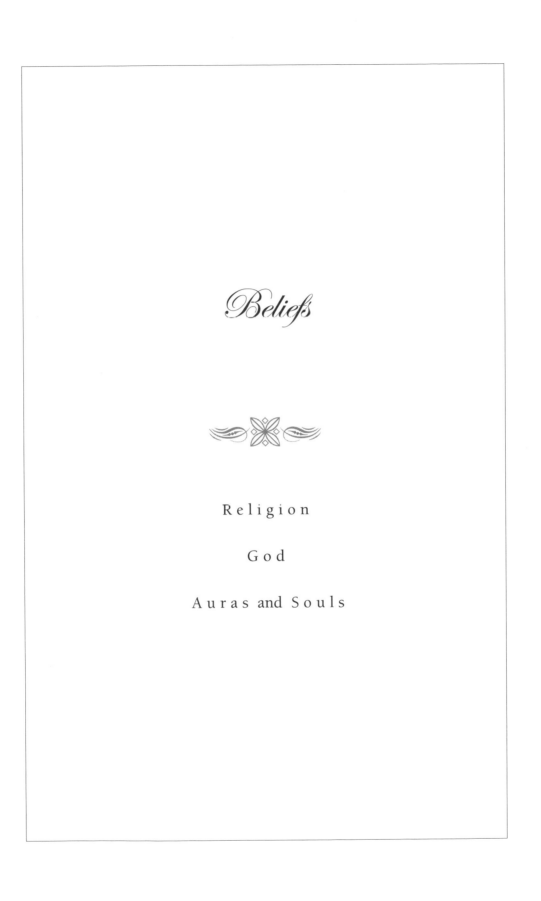

Religion

God

Auras and Souls

~R e l i g i o n~

Priel:

Since early cognitive man, there has been the belief that a great power protects, rewards and punishes. Cavemen sat in their caves imagining a god of fire. Indians stood on mountain tops calling to Mother Nature. Greeks stared at the stars naming families of gods in the sky. Popes and cardinals ask their saints to intercede with God to give them wisdom. Religions from all times are mankind's struggle to feel secure, and to derive benefits. They have come up with all kinds of ideas and theories, with rules and practices to make them all work, and have fought over minute details. There are similarities in the paths of religions. Those being a special place of worship, a high leader, rituals, and offerings and appeasements to a deity.

You are an exceptionally devout Christian. You come from the patriarchal family which, for over 400 years, has held the hereditary position for the ascension of a male member to become the highest leader of all your churches, patriarch of the orthodox Assyrian Church of the East. Still, I know you embrace many ideas and beliefs from other faiths and philosophies. Can we follow the trail of the major religions which have most influenced the world?

Ashoorian:

Since there is strong evidence that there were complex religions at least six thousands years ago, it might be that some were influential as they were spread by migration or conquerors. However, we should only discuss with certainty those which have been in some way recorded in antiquity.

Priel:

Is there a particular order to follow?

Ashoorian:

It's difficult to have an order. Let us just go first as far into the early history as we can, before we talk of organized religions with specified rules and detailed group observances. I should say that religion as a concept appeared at the time when civilizations started and religious structures were built. Remember that religion is a manmade word. Religion for primitive cavemen was completely different and mysterious. Not the way modern man is imagining.

Let us think about primitive caveman sitting in his cave imagining a great spirit fire, which was not comprehensible to him. He started imagining and creating kinds of deities and invisible forms which he unconsciously was invoking for his protection. Visualize for a few moments, him sitting in the deep darkness of midnight with his family and staring at the fire shadows dancing on the cave's walls like an invisible ghost, amid the sound of storm and thunder mixed with howls of wild animals outside the cave. Just picture his condition and the level of his fear and anxiety at that critical time.

Priel:

Do you mean, as he became conscious, he started creating some invisible forces for his protection?

Ashoorian:

I would say, yes, conscious to a certain degree. But unconscious of creating a kind of thought form to feel secure and protected. Probably, this was a new age and a new transformation for primitive man after standing upright and walking on the earth.

The first thing that fascinated him at that critical time was Mother Nature. He felt the power of it all around himself. He observed and witnessed the life and death on the earth. He felt the nourishment of nature, the different seasons, the living and dying of creatures, plants, and his own race. For him those were all related to the mother of nature…the giver and source of life. For thousands of years he was experiencing the struggle of his hard life. Then, sometime in the eon he came to realize that everything comes from Mother Nature's womb, and goes back again, to be recycled and reborn. This might be one of the main factors and causes for the appearance of a female creator, or goddess.

It has been written that early Native Americans would not break a small branch of a tree without getting permission from the concerning tree. When they were going to set up their tents, they would get permission from the earth to dig a hole. They would pray for the soul of the animals they were to kill for food. Such a great people with such a strong connection with the mother earth are already one with the cosmic soul. In return, the universe was paying back, because they deserved it, and deserved to inherit all the knowledge and treasures of the mother earth.

As we all know, they had great masters, shamans or medicine men, who were able to perform phenomena beyond modern man's understanding. They used power of mind over matter and the earth elements. Why not. They were the most honest children of Mother Nature.

Priel:

What about shamanism? Is it possible that shamanism was the first religion of the world? Would you describe it and say where it began?

Ashoorian:

It has been said that shamanism came from the four corners of the earth. Shamanism might be one of the oldest, or parallel to paganism. However, a shaman, medicine man, whatever he would have been called in the language of his people, was a man in a tribe or primitive group who was not an ordinary man. He had a mysterious power in mind training, and held a special personality in his group. He was highly believed by his people, and they had very strong faith in his knowledge and esoteric power. He had those high essential qualities that it was believed had been inherited from his ancestors, or, some believed he had tapped those high frequencies of his own superconsciousness.

By that strong natural power he possessed, he was able to concentrate, sometimes enhanced by using some kind of drums, sounds, or dramatic chanting, and enter a different dimension through an altered state of consciousness. From there he was able to eliminate their illnesses, solve their problems, and bring forth the essential information demanded by his tribe. He had the ability to contact and acquire a mysterious knowledge to empower his people.

Priel:

When I was a child, most people laughed at anyone who made use of herbs for healing purposes. And we didn't know that one's state of mind could affect his health, or, vice versa, that a person's individual physical chemistry could affect his mind. Scientific studies have now given us better insight into natural healing. I'm thinking about how the shamans, or medicine men, had special knowledge about the use of herbs for healing, and about their ability to gain wisdom through meditation. They were blending thoughts and products of the earth to implore the universe. They must have been tremendously admired as very wise men. Although, I think you are saying that it was even more than that. A power of the mind as well. Did the primitive people see all of that as a kind of magic?

Ashoorian:

First, let's define the word magic. The word magic is derived from Greek 'maigia', which means great wisdom, or great science. During the ages of the old days, the word 'maigu' was attributed to the great masters, who were called wise men. The three wise men who visited Jesus Christ were astrologers and high priests, and were called 'magi'; one from Babylon, one from Egypt, and the other from Persia. There were hundreds of these masters in all ages of history who were called magu, or wise men.

Priel:

The typical person, and the majority of people in the United States, at least, understand the word magic to describe something in fairytales, or else as a performance of well executed tricks done in the form of entertainment.

Ashoorian:

That's true. You asked me if the primitive people thought their shamans performed magic, and it's difficult and a little bit complicated to define the performance of a shaman as a magical performance considering the modern, or Western, interpretation.

God has many good aspects in the universe. One of the greatest aspects of God has been manifested in nature. Just imagine what Mother Nature is providing us. So the forces in nature are good aspects of God. They are divine and helpful. If a shaman, or wise man, is using those forces as a medium between himself and God, with good intention, it should not be considered as magic.

The ritual that a shaman is performing is a kind of divination. To him everything is natural. His intention is just to enter into an altered state of consciousness and contact the great spirit of his ancestors, then come back with good and healthy information.

As defined by the masters of the world, a wise man is capable of causing some kind of changes to occur in conformity with will, intention, and the essence of his individual higher self, in full accord with natural cosmic law. This, unfortunately, has not been understood by modern man and his science. Magic works through a subtle invisible realm. Modern man and his science work through a tangible physical world.

Priel:

In modern times, firefighters have witnessed how Native Americans stopped wildfires that were out of control by marking a line of trees before the flames reached that point. Witnesses have seen how the wild-fire burned and destroyed everything on its path, but as soon as it reached the marked point it suddenly stopped and died off. Some firefighters in a café were observed remarking that when they had no more hope of stopping a fire, their supervisor said that it was time to bring in the Indians.

Ashoorian:

In the course of my several decades of studying different esoteric and mystical philosophies, I have learned that this kind of activity that the Native Americans have performed belongs to the great masters and sages of antiquity. People with such an ability were told that they had power over four elements of the earth, such as fire, air, water, and earth. Such powerful masters have lived all over the world and have performed extraordinary and unbelievable miracles.

Priel:

During all those ages that primitive cultures flourished in the four corners of the earth, and eventually as the high civilizations rose and actual complex religions developed, the shamans, and then later the high priests, all appear to have practiced the "great science", or magic. How would you explain magic and religion in the time of antiquity?

Ashoorian:

In the time of antiquity, religion and magic should have been considered as one, because in many ancient civilizations, religion and magic shared fundamental origins. I was reading a book about ancient Sumer a few years ago. There was a picture of a small statue of a woman with outstretched arms holding a baby. The description was, "Sumerian mother holding her sick child, and invoking the power of nature to heal her baby". I stopped reading for a moment. I visualized 4,800 years ago, a desperate Sumerian mother standing under the stars of midnight, holding her sick baby and invoking the power of the North Wind, which they believed had cool nature for healing fever and other sicknesses. At that time, that desperate mother had no idea of any kind of magic, religion, or any other philosophy. In such invocation, she was trying to attract those potential powers of life to save her child. She was drawing that power from the deep source of her soul and being. She was trying to invoke the natural power of nature to manifest healing power from a non-manifested dimension like her ancestors had done thousands of years before.

Priel:

Ancient peoples' environment was so close to nature.

Ashoorian:

They learned to invoke the power of nature for different demanded subjects. They learned how to communicate the spirit of right law in the nature, to make them interact in accordance with their will for healing, purification, and protection from unfriendly and hostile spirits. This type of divination has been used in the different nations and cultures over the world. Unfortunately, after the fall of the great empires of antiquity, this great science fell into the hands of ordinary men. Since then, it has been misunderstood, misused, and abused for ages.

Priel:

People in isolated, undeveloped areas have had simple ideas and social structures. There are still isolated groups in parts of the world today who practice shamanism and forms of magic. As civilizations developed, with their magnificent edifices, sophisticated art and language, and rules of government, what happened to their worship?

Ashoorian:

Most of us know that organized and complex religions began in civilized cultures along with all the other structure and regulations a large society develops. They grew more extensive and specific in their beliefs and hierarchies. They went from simple outdoor mountaintop gatherings, to actual constructed mountain-like pyramids with stairs leading up to a platform on top. These all were used mostly for festivals, offerings to their deities, and initiations, and were the most important places for a society for several thousand years. Similar remains of them are all over the world. Eventually, their beliefs and hierarchies became more extensive, and the places of worship became ornate temples.

Priel:

One practical reason for their building on high mounts was probably to enable large masses of people to view the activities. But, do you think they elevated their worship places in order to be closer to their gods, as a carry over from the primitive people worshipping on mountaintops?

Ashoorian:

That makes a lot of sense. It seems that high lands had a different atmosphere for worship. Some primitive people believed that mountains had a quality of divine essence and special sacredness. Really, who doesn't feel transcended, meditating quietly on a mountaintop?

Priel:

Let's mention a few of the most known, early organized religions, and talk about goddesses, paganism and pantheons.

Ashoorian:

Basically, in very earliest history, there existed only one belief which humanity embraced. That was of a supreme goddess as female creator of the universe. Some scholars have stated that this was continuous from more than 15,000 B.C. In scriptures and documents from thousands of years ago, goddesses were influential in different corners of the world. In Sumer, she was called Inanna. In Egypt, Isis. In Babylon, she was known as Ishtar, in Persia, Mitra, in Greece, Gaia and in Rome, she was Juno. In India, Shiva was depicted as both female and male. There is indication that there were goddesses in the Americas, Pacific Islands, and in Asia. Later on, the power of the female deity became reduced, and even eliminated in some nations, in favor of great masculine deities.

Priel:

In some nations there became a profusion of gods and goddesses for all kinds of functions or powers. A pantheon. Some gods had wives and children as well. Often, a city had its own personal god over the city. Gods and goddesses were all around the world for thousands of years, and modern man and scholars are confused by the variety of them who are similar in character but with different names. For instance, numerous religions had a sun god. Can it be possible that they were the same god adopted from various cultures and simply having different names because of language translations?

Ashoorian:

It's feasible considering the close proximity of the cultures at those times. Sometimes the names were of a descriptive nature, or symbolic, so would be entirely different. Even a translation of a given name would sound different. But character wise they are mostly the same. Shamesh of Sumer, and Ra of Egypt, were sun gods, as well as Tonatiuh of the Aztecs, and many others. Zecharia Sitchin did exceptional research for his many detailed books. He wrote, "We have entered the temples of the Greeks, and the Aryans, the Hittites and the Hurrians, the Canaanites, the Egyptians, and the Amorites. We have followed paths that took us across continents and seas, and clues that carried us over several millennia. And all the corridors of all the temples have led us to one source: Sumer."

Priel:

There was one very early deity who had many names within his own nation. Would you tell about Marduk?

Ashoorian:

To the Sumerians and Babylonians, the deity Marduk was considered the founder of the heaven and earth. That was why he was given such a high rank among all their other gods. He was so revered that 50 different names were given to him, each for a different aspect of life. The names had different signs and special powers. The only person who had permission to summon the worship rituals for him was the high priest of the temple. The priest had to transcend himself to a high state of his superconsciousness, and gain a special power to perform the essential rituals for the temple.

Priel:

The similarity of priests' functions to those of shamans' is perhaps a carry over isn't it?

Ashoorian:

It's entirely possible. I wish there was a way I could peek back into history at the moment a high priest was performing that kind of ritual. What a fantastic pleasure it could be for me to witness the summoning of the great Assur, deity of my Assyrian ancestors. Eventually, some religions began to evolve from the pantheons to one-god beliefs.

Priel:

I'm still thinking of all the costly temples those nations built for their gods or god. When we think about King Solomon's riches with 40,000 stalls of horses for his chariots, and the cities he built to house them and his 12,000 horsemen, it is easy to imagine the temple he built, which is said to have been overlaid with gold.

Ashoorian:

Huge populations required a greater area for congregating. Wealthy nations could provide gold, marble, and precious gems for the adornment of their gods' homes. Rulers like Solomon, and pharaohs, wanted to please their gods, and also they wanted to build on a grand scale to impress the populace as being their great representative to their god. It gave them tremendous power over the people.

Priel:

Far later, during the grandiose Renaissance, along came the most magnificent of all religious edifices, those colossal, enormous Cathedrals with their exquisite art and craftsmanship of both interior and exterior. The question has always been that after all the historical events, and the magnificence, passion, and wealth of religions, was anything benefited from that splendor of the past?

Ashoorian:

Possibly, nothing. As the great Sufi masters liked to say, "All these shall pass." In fact, as we have witnessed the history, all those splendors of the past have gone! The great temples of pharaohs, the wealth and treasures of King Solomon, and the extravagant structures of worship throughout the world have been destroyed and their ruins have scorched under the heat of the sun. Their memories have been buried under desert sand storms during the course of time, and most of all through destruction by the hands of aggressive men of different nations.

It has been said that whatever is constructed, is subject to destruction, and whoever is born, is subject to die. This is a universal law. That is what has happened to all that greatness and grandeur of the past.

Priel:

So much effort, toil, and suffering throughout the ages for, and in the name of, religion is really very sad. Where do we stand now? What is our position at such a critical time of the twenty first century, the century of space and science? Will people move out of the old bondage of religion toward a new transformation of enlightenment?

Ashoorian:

We already are on the right path toward perfection. We and our ancestors have been witness to the old religions, and especially in the last two millennia, the newer religions. Despite all the dogmatisms of today's religions, we still have the messages of great prophets and spiritual masters to guide us on our divine journey to our ultimate perfection… which is happening in the fifth dimension.

Priel:

As the fifth dimension progresses further, with all the high technology on one hand, and the influence of the new religions on the other, what kind of impact is mankind expected to experience?

Ashoorian:

Any kind of impact finally will be reconciled. Religions have no choice but to bend and be flexible to the new age of science and the new way of spirituality.

Priel:

How can that be reconciled in the old religions, like Hinduism, one of the oldest religions still in existence, and Judaism, as well as Buddhism, Christianity, Islam, and some even more recent ones, considering the influence that they have over their nations?

Is it happening in these times that the majority of people in those faiths are becoming to view their teachings as simple guidance for peace and harmony in life, while only a minority are still entangled in the literal interpretations ruled down by sometimes confused or despotic leaders?

Ashoorian:

Your assumption could be fairly close to what is and will be happening. Now, you asked me quite a while ago to speak about some of the major religions which are influencing us today.

The Hindu religion has existed for thousands of years, possibly before many other religions from the time of antiquity. Some believe that Hinduism is so ancient that its origin is lost in the mist of prehistory, and Hindus themselves believe that their religion has existed forever. There are many scriptures, legends, and myths about this religion, which is called the mother of all the current religions.

Priel:

Some people believe that Hindu tradition is primitive and superstitious, because of the worship of so many deities and idols.

Ashoorian:

Well, in fact, they should not think that. The Hindu understanding of

God is incredible and sophisticated, and does not have any aspects of superstition in its philosophy.

Priel:

Hinduism is one of the most influential religions of the ancient and modern worlds. Would you please explain its philosophy and core beliefs?

Ashoorian:

I'll try to explain some which are more known in today's world. For example, Hinduism believes in a trinity of gods. These three gods are Brahma, as creator of universe, Vishnu, as protector and supreme beyond any form, and Shiva, as destroyer or liberator. Shiva is very popular in India. He is famous for a graceful dance in a halo of flame, with a ball of fire in one hand and a small drum in the other, representing the start and end of the present cycle of the universe.

Priel:

Why is it, despite multiple deities and also a type of animism, that Hinduism remains so acceptable to followers today?

Ashoorian:

Because their oldest scripture, Veda, written more than 4,000 years ago, is about exceedingly sweet hymns to their gods, nature, and the ultimate existence of the world. Regarding the many gods, for instance those painted in temples, wise men and educated Hindus never take the images literally. They see and revere in them the divine essence and real aspect of God. Besides, they believe that God is not only to be worshiped, but to be experienced as well. Opinions criticizing Hindu gods have been written, but beyond what those people think, Hindu gods have mysterious allegorical and metaphorical purposes.

Priel:

After the Veda and other Hindu scriptures, what about their *Bhagavad-Gita*?

Ashoorian:

It is a thrilling epic poem of ultimate wisdom. From the point of view of literature and philosophy, Gita is the most important and influential of all their religious writings. In my opinion, whoever wants to seek spirituality should read the Gita. It talks about Krishna, the great avatar, who gives advice in the battlefield to his disciple, Arjana, to go to war. The battlefield is symbolic. The war is between human being and his ego. Krishna's advice is an inspiring model for humanity. The Gita poetically gives the basic idea of human philosophy about karma, reincarnation, and yoga and its teachings. It is not for Hindus only. It is for everyone who desires conscious awareness of God. Gita's wisdom applies to all nations of the world.

Priel:

Hinduism embraces meditation, yoga, and the idea of reincarnation, all of which you have mentioned just now and which we can address later. But, at this time, can you please give a good description of an avatar?

Ashoorian:

Before I describe an avatar, you should hear a few lines from the Gita that Krishna is answering his disciple, Arjana, who asks Krishna, "Who are you? Are you one of those who was born after the lawmaker of the world?" Krishna responds:

"I have had many embodiments and so have you. All of them I remember, but yours, you do not, though I am in a spiritual unborn and my true self am imperishable. Though I am (in a cosmic sense) the controller of all the creatures; establishing myself in my own nature, I come into manifest form through my own nature, I come into manifest form through my own magicalpower. Whenever there is a decline of righteousness and a rise of unrighteousness, I send forth myself as a man among men for the protection of the good, for the destruction of the wicked, for the establishment of righteousness. I come into the expression from age to age." (5-8)

There is an amazing similarity between Jesus' words, and those of Krishna and Buddha. Particularly when he says, "I am alpha and omega," —the beginning and the end. Or, when he says, "Whoever believes in me will have eternal life which is imperishable...", and so forth. These are in the words of all the great masters and avatars who believe that everything in the universe is one. Their final and ultimate teachings are about oneness of the universe.

Priel:
How do scholars and spiritual masters define the nature, or characteristics, of avatars?

Ashoorian:
It is considered that the mystery of an avatar is his birth, life, and resurrection. He is the reincarnation of God's essence, a divine embodiment and anointed soul, or the messiah soul, who comes into the world in the form of a human. An avatar, which in Sanskrit means 'descended', is completely self realized, detached from all earthly pleasures and desires. He is identified as a universal supreme spirit. To an avatar, taking a body and leaving it is a matter of small consequence. He knows and remembers all his reincarnations, while other, ordinary people, forget

their past embodiment. All the avatars are conscious of living forever with or without their body. They have reached the highest level of enlightenment through meditation. Past, present, and future are one for avatars. To them, everything under the sun is subject to decaying and dying. They know the universal reality that a seed should die to grow and bring forth the fruit and essence of its originality. Whenever the world consciousness turns dark, one or a number of these perfect souls will come to the world to set the way for cleaning the darkness from the planet. The real prophets are a metaphor of a seed that brings forth fruit. The prophets are the seed, and the results of their teachings are the fruit.

Priel:

Buddha is considered an avatar. As we know, Buddhism was born and emerged out of Hinduism. How did that happen?

Ashoorian:

In short, about 2,500 years ago, the Hindu prince, Sidharta Guatama, wanted to know why there was such misery in the world. He left the castle and abandoned all the comforts and position of his royal family, joining some great Indian sages in order to learn the answer. He followed the desert and forest fakirs for many years, wandering from place to place, adhering to their strict teachings of meditation through deprivation and fasting. He was never arriving at any enlightenment.

At last, one day while he was sitting in meditation under a now famous tree, he heard the voice of a master teaching his student a musical instrument. The master said, "If you wind the strings too tight, the sound will be out of tune. And if you leave them too loose, it will be worse. To get the best sound out of your instrument, tune it in the middle of these two levels."

The legend says that the prince was spontaneously enlightened. He opened his eyes and went to the river and washed his face. He asked a shepherd to give him something to eat. He was awakened. 'Buddha', means 'the awakened one'. He reached the highest level of self realization. He realized that self denial is not the route to enlightenment. He realized that the path to spirituality is when one is awakened and goes back to the public to serve them with the wisdom he attained. Buddha left the masters, and for many years wandered through India gathering followers. For 2,500 years, love and compassion have been Buddhism's core belief, and impermanence, the cornerstone of their religion.

Priel:

Since it grew into a huge religion, he must have been talking about more than enlightenment. Did he formulate that core philosophy and other ideas which caused the actual religion to occur?

Ashoorian:

He did. He developed the idea that everything we perceive by our senses and illusions is impermanent. In fact, impermanency is the core belief of Buddhism. Most important of all, he developed the Four Noble Truths, and the Eight Fold Paths to enlightenment.

Priel:

Would you please briefly state them?

Ashoorian:

The Four Noble Truths have been stated in Buddhism almost as follows:

- Life if suffering, characterized as incomplete and unsatisfactory.
- Life is suffering and miserable due to attachment of humans to their worldly desires.
- There is a way for an end to suffering. A way to detach ourselves from all the unwanted desires of the earthly world.

- The way, or path, is spirituality and meditation which will liberate and guide us to the Eight Fold Paths.

These Eight Fold Paths are very important and essential in the life of Buddhist followers, and they can definitely be helpful to all people. They are the Right view, Right thought, Right speech, Right action, Right livelihood, Right effort, Right mindfulness, and Right concentration. Of course, each is self explanatory. For example, the first path is how to view life, the second is to consider our thoughts before expressing ourselves, and the third means speech will reveal our real character in our action and livelihood. The last two paths, mindfulness and concentration, are particularly emphasized by Buddhists. They remind their followers that whatever they do, or any action they take, must be done with mindfulness and concentration. They believe if one acts in his life according to the Four Noble Truths, and firmly considers the Eight Fold Paths, it will be the final liberation toward enlightenment and nirvana.

Priel:

Since Buddhism's foundation is based on Hinduism, why are there differences in some of their philosophies?

Ashoorian:

There are significant issues upon which they do not agree. For example, Buddhist's do not believe in a deity as creator of the universe. They maintain that from primordial time there existed a kind of elements which had potentiality for the creation. And they believe these primordial elements existed from eternal time with no beginning and no end. For this reason, most of the scholars have considered Buddhism half religion and half philosophy.

Priel:

This kind of belief would be strange to western man. Besides, it has been said that every cause has an effect, and each effect, a cause. What do they think was the cause of those primordial elements and their potentiality for the creation of our existing universe?

Ashoorian:

Buddhism firmly believes that infinite powers, which collectively formed some substances, have been continuously creating and dissolving billions of universes, this particular one being ours. Let me emphasize, that they do not consider that power as a god, but just as primordial potential elements.

Priel:

One has to wonder, since they emphasize interdependence of all things in the universe, shouldn't they somehow think those primordial potential elements would be dependent upon something as well?

Ashoorian:

That is the reason why some have considered Buddhists to be atheists. To describe this conflicting point between the two religions needs many pages. However, I'll try to cut it short and simple. Buddhists believe that nothing has a solid identity, that everything is dependent upon other things. But, on the contrary, Hindus believe in a supreme, pure intelligence, which they call Brahma, to be the cause and creator of the universe.

Priel:

So, since Buddhists believe nothing can be the cause of itself, they ask to whom, and on what is the Hindu creator Brahma dependent upon.

Ashoorian:

That's it. Hindus maintain that an absolute entity, which is pure aware-ness, cannot be cognitive and is beyond our comprehension. Therefore, it does not need to be dependent upon anything to exist. This is so very meaningful and allegorical for creation, which we talked about on previous pages. Aside from all of this, however, Buddhists and Hindus both believe in the continuity and dissolution of the universe.

Priel:

Then, as you have told, they both say that before anything happened, there was a pure consciousness to guide the evolution toward intelli-gence. And now that we have discussed these two major religions, why don't we talk about another ancient religion which exists still today. That, is Zoroastrian.

Ashoorian:

Zoroastrian emerged in Persia (Iran) around the time of Hammurabi, circa eighteenth century B.C. Although, some believe he was contempo-rary with Buddha around 500 B.C. It is stated Zoroaster was one of the first monotheistic preachers, the son of a pagan priest. In the ancient time they claimed he was their messiah. He believed the universe has an invisible architect as a creator. He was inspired by a divine perception of the spirit, which he called Ahura Mazda.

It was said that when Zoraster was a child he had the ability to calm wild beasts, and to remember all of his reincarnations. He lived in the wilderness as an aesthetic, sleeping in caves, and giving reverence to all living creatures.

Priel:

He spent ten years traveling to other regions, preaching in the name of the one god, Ahura Mazda. What are the basics of what he taught?

Ashoorian:

Ancient people believed that in all the universe the blood of life was the most precious sacrificial offering. Zoroaster reversed that idea, saying that for being with Ahura Mazda, there is no need to conduct sacrifices.

He talked about twin spirits as negative and positive forces in the universe by which all the world came into existence. He considered these two polarities of energy as holy living fire. He also believed in a continuing process of the universe like the Hindus and Buddhists do.

Priel:

Are there Zoroastrian scriptures?

Ashoorian:

Yes, there are. The Avesta evolved, and consists of 17 Gathas, or hymns, about the principals of life and worshipping God. Surprisingly, from three of those hymns, it is believed the Buddhist's Eight Fold Paths were taken—the Right View, the Right Speech, and the Right Thought. Most of all, their scripture is believed to be the first sacred writing about life after death.

Priel:

The majority of Zoroastrians today are in Iran and the Middle East.

Ashoorian:

That's right. Even now, Iranians display on beautiful scripted plaques in their homes and businesses the three principals of the Right View, Right Speech, and Right Thought. And Zoroastrians still, today, keep a fire burning in their temples. It is the same flame from the ancient times, which they call the Holy Living Fire.

Priel:

The other religion of today which has ancient roots is that of Judaism. Abraham, the Sumerian from Mesopotamia, left his home in the city of Ur, taking with him his tribe, their traditional Sumerian religion, and also the new concept of only one god. The story of his travels is one of the most famous of all times. What will you tell about that?

Ashoorian:

It was around 3,000 years B.C. that Abraham began his journey to locate the "Promised Land", a land of milk and honey, which his god had promised him. Jews believe that this was the beginning of their patriarchal Jewish religion. So much has been written about Abraham and his descendents, their troubles, the places they settled, and the battles they won and lost. Oral histories they told contained that information and also many prophesies. The most dramatic phase of their religion arose about 1,400 B.C., when their leader, Moses, received a message from their god. Cut into stone, the message gave them ten rules, or comandments, to follow in order to please him, Jehova (Yahwey in Hebrew).

Priel:

Those rules are very like some of the laws inscribed on Hammurabi's monument in Babylon of Mesopotamia from his reign around 1,700 B.C. The similarity is intriguing, although Hammurabi had many more laws, including some pertaining to civic and trading affairs.

Ashoorian:

That is so. It is thought that there were actually two sets of the Jewish Ten Commandments. An earlier set being about rituals and dietary observances, and the second one about moral ethics.

Priel:

One school of thought is that they were both given to Moses at the same time. However, the ethical sayings are the ones most observed today, also by Christians and Moslems as well, with all sects writing them in variations of wording according to their own understanding and interpretations. Basically, they say to:

> Have no other God
> Don't worship any form of idolatry
> Use the name of God well
> Observe the Sabbath
> Honor your parents
> Don't murder
> Don't commit adultery
> Don't steal
> Don't mislead with false words
> Don't covet what others have

Ashoorian:

You mentioned Hammurabi's laws. Abraham's people had carried down some of the old laws, or practices, from their Mesopotamian days, and had absorbed others from the many lands in which they had resided. They eventually wrote some books of their own which contained a multitude of detailed instructions concerning most aspects of their lives.

The main book, the Torah, originally applied to the five books of Moses. Now the Torah is sometimes regarded as including the collections of their ancient oral stories eventually put into text and now called the Old Testament. The Torah also includes their entire body of Jewish law. There is a body of rabbinic literature called the Talmud, which contains an enormous compilation of laws, and of discussions revolving around the laws. Jewish observances of Biblical law have been determined by interpretation of the Talmud.

Priel:

Their prophets of old had dramatic predictions. Of course, the prophesy with the most impact on the religion was about the coming of a savior to deliver them from their many travails. In fact, they still anticipate that arrival of that messiah, or in Aramaic, 'mshikha'.

Ashoorian:

Messiah, incidentally, means an expected, consecrated (anointed) deliverer. The word Christ is the Greek translation of 'mshikha'.

Priel:

They had a number of messiahs come and go, some being accepted for a while. The one most famous, and who has had a colossal impact on world civilization is, of course, Jesus of Nazareth, born in the land of Judah during the time of Roman occupation. He was said to have been of an immaculate conception according to God's plan.

Ashoorian:

Jesus taught a message of love and peace, and to treat others as you would like to have them treat you. He was against the strict and often cruel interpretations of the laws of the high priests, and promoted a simpler and gentler way much the same as Buddha and Zoroaster did. As a young boy, in discussions at the temple he amazed the priests with his stunning knowledge of the laws, and with his ability to heal and perform a kind of miracles, a word derived from Latin meaning 'to wonder at'.

Priel:

Most of the world has heard of the nativity and crucifixion of Jesus. There also is a lot about him that many people haven't heard, isn't there?

Ashoorian:

Well, there are more books to the New Testament than were put into the King James version. The missing gospels told about his family and childhood, and the lost years before he began his mission in Palestine preaching the message he said God had sent him to do. Some scholars think those earlier years were spent in Tibet, India, and other countries.

Priel:

Are there any writings from that time which pertain to that?

Ashoorian:

There are some books about Jesus' journeys through the Silk Road, Nepal, and Tibet with the help of the Essenes. There were some writings there about a great master, a compassionate teacher and healer, by the name of Isu, who had disciples wherever he went. Monks have shown his name in their own scriptures, and with honor have said: Yes, your saint Isu was here.

His Aramaic name was 'Eshu'. The Greek translation was 'Iesous', and the Late Latin is Jesu, and Jesus. However, just let me say that all these writings have not been universally verified. What is accountable is his divine message. He was aware of his destiny of dying and resurrecting. He knew that his universal teaching was the golden truth for all the nations. In addition, Jesus was a great master of Cabbalah and alchemy. He was an alchemist who was able, instead of converting base metal to pure gold, to transform his physical human nature to the highest source of divinity and become one with the cosmic soul. His message of love your neighbor like yourself is eternal and absolute compassion for all mankind, and applies to all the nations of the world.

Priel:

Aramaic was the language spoken by Jesus, his family, and those in that region of Palestine, as well as by his apostles and some of the first writers of the New Testament. Aramaic is your native language. Is it possible to give a simple history of that language?

Ashoorian:

Aramaic is a Mesopotamian language still spoken today. It was the language of Aramaia. Because of its smooth sounds and beauty of words, it was adopted by all of the areas of Mesopotamia, varying only by regional dialects. For example, the tribe of Abraham acquired the dialect which came to be called Hebrew. There are brilliant explanations of the Aramaic language and its dialects translated by the Assyrian theological scholar, Dr. George M. Lamsa, in his book, *The Modern New Testament from the Aramaic*.

The conquests and occupations by the Assyrians and Babylonians spread the Aramaic all over the Middle East beginning circa 700 B.C. Eventually, there were four main dialects. In the west, from Syria through Palestine there was a Northern and a Southern dialect. To the east, in Mesopotamia, was also a different Northern dialect, spoken by the Assyrians, and a different Southern dialect, spoken by Babylonians. However, now Aramaic is just considered to have East and West dialects.

Priel:

The Jews were known as Hebrews until the kingdom of Judah, one of the regions where they lived in Palestine, became dominant. Then, they also came to be called Judeans, and Jews is a derivative. But, didn't Hebrew become a dead language once during those times?

Ashoorian:

When Jesus was born, Hebrew was almost an unspoken language.

Priel:

Within the Jews there were several variations in religious philosophies, or sects, of the faith, such as the Pharisees, Sadducees, Zealots, and Essenes.

Ashoorian:

Just like today, for instance, there are different sects of Judaism and Christianity.

Priel:

Jesus' mother belonged to the group called Essenes, and she was from the hereditary family of the priesthood. Probably, Jesus might have been influenced by them. Would you tell us something about the Essenes?

Ashoorian:

Not only was Jesus influenced by the Essenes, but so was his cousin, John the Baptist, who was also from a family of Essenes. As many scholars of old and modern times have stated, Essenes were a Jewish brotherhood. They called themselves the White Brotherhood, which symbolized purity and righteousness, and they lived in great harmony, men and women together. They embraced a more simple and pure manner of living and worshiping, preferring to live in the countryside away from the rigid temple priests of large cities.

Priel:

How did it begin, and what was their tenet?

Ashoorian:

Its real beginning is not known. Their teachings were very sophisticated and emphasized practicing spirituality through purity of the soul, mind and body. It is believed that they practiced an early system of yoga, which consisted of different kinds of body movements for receiving cosmic forces.

Priel:

Weren't they also well known for healing ?

Ashoorian:

They did feed and help travelers who needed help. They had great masters who were able to act according to universal right law for performing miracles and healing in their daily life. They believed that if mankind tuned to his higher self and divine forces, it would enable him to achieve a very high level of self mastery and power of mind over matter. They believed their meditation should be concentrated on specific angels to assist them in that kind of performing.

Priel:

How was their meditation concentrated on specific angels?

Ashoorian:

In their philosophy there was a symbolic tree of knowledge, which had seven branches stretched upward representing seven heavenly forces, or angels, and seven roots stretched downward, representing earthly forces. Their meditation depended upon what subject or idea they had in mind to manifest. The angels had names, and to each one a specific power was attributed. A person would concentrate on the concerning angel who was in accordance with the subject demanded by them.

Priel:

Was the White Brotherhood known in other regions?

Ashoorian:

Their philosophy and teaching spread to China, Tibet, Egypt, India, and other regions. In fact, traditional Judaism has given a theory that the Essenes were followers of Enoch, father of Methusela. Most important of all, Essenes believed that there were to be two messiahs to come. One, as a teacher, and the other, as a king. They later thought John the Baptist was the teacher, and Jesus the king.

However, little was known of this brotherhood until the last findings of the Dead Sea Scrolls in 1947, from which there was considerable information about them. The scrolls validated many subjects of the Old Testament, particularly the prediction of Isaiah about Jesus Christ and his birth, teachings, crucifixion, and resurrection.

Priel:

So much is said about the Jews rejecting Jesus as their messiah. Of course, some did accept him and were his earliest followers. Since he was in disfavor with the priests, some potential followers might have been intimidated to openly express support for him. Also, there had been other self-proclaimed messiahs not long before him.

Ashoorian:

Besides all you said, there was one great reason for the priests and the majority of the Jewish nation to reject him. It was the law of their religion, which was being practiced for almost 1,350 years before Jesus was born. The Jewish requirement was that a rabbi must be 30 years of age to be permitted to preach in a temple, he should be married, and should have a son to follow his mission. I think Jesus was 30 years old when he preached in temples, but was not married and had no son. So, in fact, from the Jewish point of view, he was not qualified. And, he was a radicalist. He was breaking their law by working and healing on the Sabbath. He prevented women from being stoned, he spoke against the fundamental rituals and rules of dogmatic religion, and devalued the system of their priesthood. How could that great hierarchy of priests tolerate that! But, more than anything else, they were saying that he claimed to be the son of God. When, in fact, he did not mean a physical son of God, but a spirit child of God. Because, he believed that all of mankind are the children, or the creation, of God.

Priel:

Christian belief is that even though he was a Jew, the prophets never meant that a messiah was to come only for the Jews, but to come from the Jews to be a messiah for all.

Ashoorian:

The ultimate truth of his intention was not like any other Israelite prophet to lead and teach only his own nation. He had unconditional love even for his enemies. His messages were universal. A real messiah is an avatar, and an avatar has a universal Christ soul. For them, all of mankind are the children of God. For them, every creature and human being has the same aspect of God. That was the reason why Jesus Christ told his disciples to go to the four corners of the world and preach his words.

Priel:

In reading the scriptures of the Old and New Testaments, there is much which can be traced geographically and historically, and much which sounds preposterous. Don't you think those old stories told by mouth for so many centuries before scribes wrote them down underwent changes? For instance, children on a playground can witness the same event, and yet have different impressions and choices of words when they relate the event. Then, when each new recipient of the information forms his own impressions, and uses his own words, it would be that after dozens of narrations nothing would be exactly accurate about the subject. Isn't that what happened to those old Hebrew stories, and then the scribes wrote what they thought was correct? I'm always thinking about how students of the scriptures could be confused and misled by very conscientious and devoted translators, because of words which sound the same, or because of translators' lack of knowledge about local idioms. For example, in English, the noun 'rose' is a flower, yet another English word spelled and sounding the same is the verb 'rose', which would be used as in a man 'rose' from his chair.

Ashoorian:

Sadly, many people attempt to learn and follow the scriptures literally, and they are basing their religion and behavior on specifics which are incorrect and sometimes even fought over. Alexander the Great made a celebration for the deity, Marduk. The Aramaic word 'Eda', meant 'festival', and it also meant 'hand'. What actually happened was that Alexander held the 'festival' of Marduk. The translation was that Alexander held the 'hand' of Marduk. A colossal difference.

Priel:

Your native language being Aramaic, you've been able to read the New Testament in Aramaic, its most accurate account. Does much of today's New Testament, after the many translations, differ from the Aramaic version?

Ashoorian:

There are more highly significant differences than merely translations, but I'll give you a few examples of translation errors. Take the Aramaic word 'gumlah', which means both 'rope' and 'camel'. Jesus was giving an analogy, and said that it was easier for a 'rope' to go through the eye of a needle, than for a rich, materialistic man to get into heaven. For ages people have thought Jesus was talking about trying to put a 'camel' through a needle. Now it's the same idea, because getting either a rope or a camel through a needle is impossible. In this case it is a benign error, but an example that taking everything literally can be confusing at a minimum.

Another translation error more important is some of Jesus' last words. For centuries people thought he cried out at his crucifixion, asking God why he had forsaken him. What he really said was, "Eli, Eli, Imana Shabachthani!", which means, "My God, my God, for this I was kept!"

Particularly, idioms were not understood when later translations were made. Even among the various Aramaic dialects, idioms were confusing. For example, Jesus was speaking in his Northern Aramaic dialect to the high priest, Nicodemus. He used the idiom, "born again", which meant to become like a child again. Nicodemus, who spoke a different dialect, took it literally, and could not understand how a man could return to his own mother's womb.

Priel:

Originally, wasn't the New Testament just a collection of epistles written by the apostles of Jesus?

Ashoorian:

Yes. It wasn't called the New Testament at first. The Assyrian King Abgar, in his royal capital of Edessa, had an incurable illness. Having heard about Jesus' healings without medicines, he wrote a letter to him offering to share his kingdom if Jesus would come heal him. Jesus responded that he couldn't go because he was involved with accomplishing his mission. He said he would send a disciple who could help Abgar if he had the faith to be healed. As a result of that, King Abgar was cured. He proclaimed that henceforth his nation would renounce all gods and become a nation which followed the teachings of Jesus. That was the first Christian king and nation. Written evidence of these events is preserved and available in the Record Office at Edessa from that time until now, including the actual letters.

The first gospels, which had remained continuously in the hands of Jesus' disciples throughout the first century, were most likely made for the first time into a compilation in Edessa. It was the original Eastern text of both the New and Old Testaments, called the 'Peshitta' (simple). It was written in the purest of all Aramaic dialects, which became the literary language of both East and West and remains so today. A few centuries later Rome made a new collection of the gospels. When the Edessans and other parts of the world read what had resulted, they were stunned. Not only had some books been deleted, but, even more shocking to them, there were changes and additions which no one knew where they came from.

Priel:

I watch the television ministers attempting explanations of particular scriptures. Still, after several thousand years, nobody has the answers? The popes change their minds all the time. The Mormon leaders keep coming up with new edicts. Why wouldn't any average person, who is not completely gullible, or has not been brought up in the narrow borders of his family's church, be skeptical of the rules and authoritative teachings and interpretations of religions?

Ashoorian:

People should keep open minds and search for themselves.

Priel:

So many different Christian sects have arisen, and Jesus' lessons have gone in so many directions. What would Jesus have thought to see all that mankind has done to his simple teaching?

Ashoorian:

My goodness, Ms. Priel. What an interesting thought you have had. Certainly he would have said, "Father forgive them, for they know not what they do". Yes, there is no doubt that these would surely have been his words. He died on the cross to prove his universal message to love and forgive.

He was living beyond our time and space. His mind had no boundaries. For him there was no black and white, no good and bad, and no duality. He was looking at the universe and all its creatures as a divine aspect of God. He was pure Christ's soul in Jesus' body. He was not born to judge and condemn, but on the contrary, his mission and doctrine were love, forgiveness, and compassion. Besides all of these, he had the pure essence of God, and as a man, he was the greatest avatar who ever walked on the earth.

Priel:

You mentioned that Jesus told his disciples to go to the four corners of the earth and teach his lessons. I recently was flipping through a Bible when I came across a passage of Jesus saying to his disciples, "All authority in heaven and on earth has been given to me. Go therefore and make disciples of all nations, baptizing them in the name of the Father and of the Son and of the Holy Spirit, teaching them to observe all I have commanded you; and lo, I am with you always, to the close of the age."

The Latter Day Saints (Mormons) believe that Joseph Smith found records on ancient tablets left in North America by Semites. They describe a prophet who told his people of the eminent birth of Jesus. The tablets were also to have contained later writings that said Jesus traveled in the Americas after his resurrection. What about that?

Ashoorian:

Indians of both North and Central America talk of a compassionate healer who traveled through the regions teaching them, and then saying that he must leave to help other people.

Priel:

Ancient, high civilizations existed in the Americas at various times. It is also known that a Semitic gene type was found in ancient skeletal remains in North America, and also in some modern Native Americans. Latter Day Saints believe ancient Jews migrated to America, and that Jesus came to America. Do you have anything to mention on the idea that Jesus was in the Americas?

Ashoorian:

Well, it is written in the Book of John, in the New Testament, that Jesus said he had to tend to other sheep not of that fold, that they would hear his voice, and all would become one flock and one shepherd. If you remember, I read to you a paragraph from "sleeping prophet" Edgar Cayce, the astounding psychic whose assertions about ancient America have been concluded to be mostly correct. He said even though Jesus Christ was crucified, and all the fluid from his body was drained because of nail holes in his hands and feet, and spear wounds in his chest, he survived and overcame death. He said all the great masters and avatars are able to overcome death and take their body to a celestial level. I, personally, believe in a universal Christ's soul, and also I believe that an avatar ascends from a gross body to an ethereal level. Therefore, I believe that a universal Christ's soul could have appeared in the Americas just as they all have claimed.

Omraam Aivanhov, the Bulgarian master, praised Jesus in a grand manner. He extolled that the second coming of Christ would be different. That the Christ is so superb and universal that under no circumstances would they be able to crucify him, because they would never find a tree large enough to make a cross for him!

The acts that Jesus did in the years of his life, to me, is like a great alchemist who, for example, could convert a base metal to gold. The worldwide teachings of Jesus as a divine heritage to humanity were a million times more valuable than all the gold an alchemist could have transformed. Because, Jesus was an alchemist for the human soul.

Priel:

As a result of Judeo-Christianity, Islam developed. It acknowledged and followed the way of the two beliefs, considering itself to be a continuation and fulfillment of the two.

Ashoorian:

Islam was the third Abrahamic religion, and appeared in the seventh century A.D. Islam believes in a sort of trinity which says Moses is the word of God, Jesus is the spirit of God, and Mohammed is the messenger of God.   In Arabia, their founder and prophet was Mohammed, from Mecca. He declared he was a messenger from God, and established certain teachings. Allah means, 'the God', in Arabic. Islam, means 'submitting to God's will', and Muslim, which is what they call themselves, is a derivative meaning, 'one who submits to God'.

Priel:

Please say a bit about Mohammed's background, and how he was inspired.

Ashoorian:

It's said that Mohammed was working as a merchant with his uncle, traveling with a caravan to Syria. There he met some Christian priests and bishops. He attended their churches, listening to their scriptures and services. Although he was illiterate, he had an outstanding memory and retained what he heard. When he returned home, he shared what he learned with his family.

He had many extraordinary experiences and visions. One day, he came home in an altered state and told his wife that he had meditated in a cave, and that Gabriel, the angel of God, took him on a journey to Seventh Heaven and back. This was the start of everything for him. Particularly, when his wife, Khadijah, hearing about his incredible journey, encouraged him on his spiritual path.

Priel:

What are the affirmations he declared?

Ashoorian:

Many rules developed in the years to follow, but most important are the Five Pillars of Faith. They are:

1. God is great
2. God is merciful and compassionate, and creator and ruler of earth and universe
3. The Day of Reckoning, coming with great rewards and horrendous punishment
4. Adherence to the Koran (Qur'an), the heavenly book compiled of Arabic revelations given to Mohammed in his lifetime
5. The brotherhood of Islam includes all people who revere Allah, his prophet Mohammed, the Koran, and the Day of Judgment

Priel:

As in most religions, reforms and differing sects arose.

Ashoorian:

One sect is the Shia. Its belief is that everything in the Koran is the exact word of God and to be taken at face value. The largest sect, and more traditional, is the Sunni, consisting of about three fourths of the world's Muslims.

Priel:

An extremely dynamic tenet Islam follows is the holy war, Jihad.

Ashoorian:

In the Koran it says if a Muslim male dies in a proclaimed holy war against nonbelievers, he will go to heaven and receive fantastic gratifications. I think various sects might define holy war differently.

Priel:

I do know that Muslims are supposed to live in an Islamic nation, but it is my understanding that it is permissible to reside in a non-Islamic state if they pursue bringing about Islam to that nation.

Ashoorian:

To a certain extent that might be so. But, besides the Jihad against non-believers, it also is stated that a person should do Jihad against his own ego to become a good Muslim. I lived for more than forty years as an Assyrian Christian in the Muslim nation of Iran. I had a lot of good Muslim friends and associates who were very nice and compassionate people.

Priel:

The people in Iran (ancient Persia) experienced in their culture for thousands of years the influence of the Zoroastrian religion, which was one of compassion. Do you think some of that was absorbed as a tradition?

Ashoorian:

Although Persia was converted to Islam, most of their old traditions are still being practiced in today's Iran. As I said earlier, they have those three major principals of the right speech, the right act, and the right thought.

Priel:

Something appears contradictory. Islam claims they believe in all the ancient prophets—Abraham, Elijah, Moses, Jesus—and that Mohammed is just the last and final one of them. But, Jesus taught that the world should love and forgive their enemies. How does Islam reconcile that with the edict for Jihad against nonbelievers?

Ashoorian:

The heart of Islam religion is to not separate the state from the religion. I don't want to be judgmental as to why Islam believes to destroy nonbelievers. But, let's go back to the time of Christianity's early days. The four books of the New Testament were written almost 2,000 years ago, and nobody knows all that has been added, eliminated, or even misinterpreted from those scriptures. Islam's Koran was written approximately 1,300 years ago, and has been interpreted at times by leaders who could not read or even speak Arabic. Adherence to literal interpretations is going to be erroneous.

Islam is not alone in its persecution of nonbelievers. Take the sayings of Jesus, "…love your neighbor like yourself…", and "…forgive your enemies…" That means pure, unconditional love and tolerance. Yet, when Rome became an all-Christian nation, it forced all citizens to become Christians. In the Dark Ages, during the Spanish Inquisitions, nonbelievers were tortured and executed by the church. Did those religious Christian leaders follow those words of Jesus for those innocent people? Now, come back to Islam. How can Jihad against non-believers comply with their second affirmation of the Five Pillars of Faith, which says God is merciful and compassionate? I don't have to answer this question. Those who are declaring war against nonbelievers should be fair and answer it to a universal understanding.

Who were nonbelievers? Jews? Christians? Zoroastrians? All these three religions believed in one god. Particularly, Jews and Christians were people of the book, the covenant. Yet, see what happened in the first quarter of the twentieth century. The Ottoman Empire, and Moslems, due to political reasons, massacred more than one million Armenians, about 800,000 Assyrians, and close to 700,000 Greeks. All those innocent people were descendents of the people of the book who were accepted by Islam's prophet. Why did the followers of the prophet commit such a terrible crime? If those criminals believed in the Day of Judgment, which is the third pillar of their faith, how are they going to stand face to face with their God on that particular day?

Priel:

There is possibly no religion in the world which has retained the first order of its philosophy and followed the edicts of its prophet. The thing most confounding to me is why people of the same faith viciously fight each other over the smallest details. New generations through the centuries with different philosophies, changing political situations and conditions, and the spread of a religion into new regions with different cultures—all would alter ideologies.

Ashoorian:

Unfortunately, each nation has designed a different mask for their god, and are eagerly imposing the mask to other nations. This is against the universal law. In fact, one should ask those fanatic religious leaders just who told them that God needs all those different masks?

Priel:

While you are on that subject, it would be interesting if you mention the twin Jesus in the vision of Kalil Gibran.

Ashoorian:

Thank you for reminding me of that. Allegorically, the experience of that great man conveys what I meant. Kalil Gibran, the great Lebanese poet, was meditating in an area called Sacred Valley. All of a sudden he saw a vision of twin Jesus Christs. He wondered why there should be two of them. He watched them conversing for a while. Curiosity made him go closer and hide behind a tree. One Jesus was saying, "...what is the difference in us?" The other Jesus, with great compassion, said, "The difference is that I am Jesus of Nazareth, and you are the Jesus of the church."

Priel:

He meant that Jesus of Nazareth was real, and simple, teaching in his sandals and sleeping under trees. But that Jesus of the church is what people have wrapped him in...their rituals, gold and accoutrements of grandiose worship, their manipulations of his words. Gibran's vision conveys what religions have done to their original prophets and their messages.

Ashoorian:

Exactly that is what Gibran meant. As Joseph Campbell, the great teacher put it,

"My little sermon to the churches of the world is this, you have got the symbols right there on the altar, and you have the lessons as well. Unfortunately, when you have a dogma telling you what kind of effect the symbol is supposed to have upon you, you are in trouble. It doesn't affect me that way, so am I a sinner? The real important function of the church is to present the symbols, to perform the rite, to let you behold this divine message in such a way that you are capable of experiencing it."

Priel:

Such practices have created blindness and resistance to all other ideas except their own dogma. One time I attended a Lutheran church's Bible study class. A woman asked why the Jews nowadays did not believe in Jesus as the messiah, since the New Testament is now available for all of them to read. I had to respond to her with a thought I had about that. I asked her if she had read the Book of Mormon. She was shocked, and answered, "No, why would I do that?" Then I asked her if she didn't think she should at least know about something that mentions Jesus. She responded that she was sure her religious beliefs are all she needs to know. I said to her, "This is probably the same reason most of today's Jews don't read the New Testament." Probably people will turn away from what doesn't fit their established religious teachings, because it is easier not to believe anything that to consider something new or uncertain.

Ashoorian:

Ms. Priel, in conclusion, I have a question for you. Of course, if you don't mind. My question will need an imaginary world completely different from our world with all it's standard rules, orders, and religions which we have, right or wrong, inherited from our ancestors and fanatically adhered to them. I want you for a few minutes to imagine the vastness of our universe with billions of galaxies and trillions of stars — a lot of which might have planets like ours. For certain they might have some sort of life similar to ours. But I am sure they do not have any of those prophets like Abraham, Zoroaster, Moses, Krishna, Buddha, Jesus and Mohammed. So, in your opinion, what kind of concept might they have about God and creation? Do they have any dogmatic belief to condemn others whose beliefs are not in accordance with theirs? Are they tearing each others' throats in order to impose it on others?

Priel:

I can only say that in your imaginary world, perhaps they would have in their DNA the qualities necessary for peace...in their heart, and, therefore, for their world. Then there might be no need for religions. We can hope that on Earth we truly are, as you said, constantly perfecting ourselves as we evolve toward a more uplifted state of awareness and love for others.

Ashoorian:

Precisely, that is what I expected to hear from you, Ms. Priel. Now, my last words about all of mankind's rigid and fanatic religious leaders are that human beings have extremely bitter memories from the terrible crimes committed in the name of God. This has caused the greatest embarrassment in the history of the human race. The memory of all those massacres have been depicted into the minds of different nations forever, and will never be forgotten or forgiven.

Priel:

There is something you have mentioned at various places in the book. It's a subject for which you have a great affinity, and which was a source for your early studies. It is the gentle and mystic Sufis. They meditate, dance, and chant themselves into an elevated spiritual state, and often are known as the 'whirling dervishes'. How did it happen that you became so drawn to Sufism?

Ashoorian:

When I was a young boy in Iran, the first time I saw them progressing along the street, singing and chanting, I was so impressed that for one week I was in a spellbound condition. After that, whenever one of them was passing on the sidewalk singing, I would leave all my friends and follow him for hours, listening to his words and heavenly voice.

They had such beautiful voices! Usually they would sing poems of Moulana Jalaluddin Rumi, the marvelous Persian poet and Sufi, or else praises from their holy Koran. It became my habit to follow them through the streets, sometimes all the way to their temples.

Priel:

Did your fascination continue as an adult? Did you ever visit or participate in their gatherings?

Ashoorian:

When I was twenty-two years old and a professional stage actor, I met some actor friends who had a connection with dervishes. Through them I met many dervishes at their temple. What fascinated me was the dervishes' attitude toward me at the meeting. I could not believe that they would even talk to a young Christian boy. But, to my surprise, when they found out that I was Christian, they became more kind and treated me differently. One of Rumi's poems describes that attitude, saying,

> "…Come, come, whoever you are,
> An unbeliever, a fire worshipper, come.
> Our convent is not of desperation.
> Even if you have broken your vows a hundred times,
> Come, come again."

Love, for the dervishes, is the key which opens the door into paradise. They say the purest essence of love has been projected into the entire universe by God. After a time, they invited me to sit with them and chant, "There is no God, but God." That was the greatest adventure of my life at that time.

Priel:

What did your people and family think about what you were doing?

Ashoorian:

Most people and my family didn't know about that. But actor friends used to call me "Misha Dervish", because I was completely changed. I became a different person. From that time on, my dreams became even more vivid and symbolic. I think that was my first experience of being intoxicated with divine awareness.

Priel:

I know some have a connection with Islam, but is Sufism a religion? Where and when did it originate?

Ashoorian:

Sufism is more of a universal philosophy. There is a freedom to their philosophy with the attitude that the path to God is open for all. They welcome all to join in most of their practices, and don't inquire about a person's faith. The Persian and Hindu Sufis, as well as some others, believe that all religions, not just the Islam religion, will lead humanity onto the real path towards the reality of divine awareness.

Now, there is a great contradiction for Sufis regarding their origin and history. Traditional Islamic Sufis believe that the teachings of Sufi's have come from prophet Mohammed. Other Sufi sects claim that Sufis existed centuries prior to the Islamic era, and that they operated differently, and were independent from Islamic scriptures and prophet Mohammed's teachings.

Priel:

What does the word 'sufi' mean?

Ashoorian:

The word has different meanings in different cultures and languages, but generally it has come to stand for purity, spirituality, mysticism, and knowledge. In the Arabic language, 'suf', means wool, or woolen cloak, and that became a common descriptive term for the holy dervish masters who wore them. The cloaks were like the ones pictured on the Christian aesthetic, John the Baptist. The dervish garments are simple, and patched, because dervishes are not lead astray by earthly desires and passions. Actually, 'dervish', in the Persian language, means someone who still is at the door of enlightenment.

Priel:

Are there considerable differences in the beliefs of the sects?

Ashoorian:

It's hard to say. Generally, the main concern of all Sufis is to purify their hearts and immerse in the creator. They engage themselves in repeating the name of God and the divine aspect. They continuously repeat their Zikr, which is, "La illaha illa llah". It translates, "There is no God but God". To them, the real Sufi is one who permanently keeps his heart purified by remembrance of God, in order to overcome the passion of his lower nature and achieve the higher state of ecstasy, called 'Hal'. That means, 'drunk from love of God'. They believe that the way to God is but one step — the step out of yourself. The goal is to reach the state of 'Fana', which is a state of annihilating the self in the presence of the divine and losing all senses. After that, should be the state of Baqa, which enables one to return to normal life in a better condition to serve humanity.

As far as differences in the sects, non-traditional Sufi sects believe that their system has a similarity with the universal philosophy and style practiced in different countries at least two thousand years prior to the

Islamic era. For example, in India there is that system of meditation on seven vital energy centers located on the human body, called Chakras. Each is for a different purpose, and they progress from a lower base to the very highest place.

The non-traditional Sufis have seven allegorical spiritual centers which they call Latiefe, and each has a different characteristic for their spiritual purposes. They are in an arch descending from the highest point of their creator, going through each one for formation of the soul, and then ascending back through the arch again to attain knowledge and God-like quality.

It's similar to Cabbalah, the Jewish mystic practice well known as the Tree of Life. It originally had seven centers, although now there are ten, each with a spiritual purpose. It represents the descending of man from the highest center to the lowest, and then ascending back again. That is to experience the real purpose of life, learning the divine wisdom and becoming one with their creator.

Priel:

Besides those similarities with the Chakra and Cabbalah teachings, what you said previously about Sufism wanting to annihilate self interest sounds like some Zen Buddhism beliefs.

Ashoorian:

There are some similarities between Sufism and Zen Budhism. Sufis endeavor to let go of all duality and individual self interest, through the knowledge of oneself and direct personal experience. This can be compared with Zen Buddism's no self interest and no duality that one should gain through self knowledge. A very well-known expression which Sufi's use is, "This too shall pass." It has a very similar meaning with the impermanency in life of Zen Buddhism. Again, Sufis say the moment of now is priceless, meaning impermanency again. That is, only the present moment we live has the accountability, and all other things will pass. Many scholars believe the core meaning of these two philosophies has a striking similarity.

Priel:

Sufism has become worldwide. Is it mystical universally, and is their attitude and conduct the same in the Western world as it is in the Middle East?

Ashoorian:

There is a basic difference between some sects of Sufism. Many wonder how could universal philosophies of different countries, which existed thousands of years before the Islamic era, belong to prophet Mohammed's teachings. It might be that Sufis have brought with them these older philosophies, and later on some added the philosophy of Islam.

Priel:

In general, it seems like all the sects more or less have the same belief. As you said, they believe that chanting the name of God purifies their heart toward their creator. Isn't purity the main purpose of the Sufis worldwide?

Ashoorian:

Yes, chanting and dancing and whirling to become one pointed on God, opening the door to their soul towards divine awareness of the creator. They have said that when they chant, the chanter, the chanting, and the subject of the chanting, which is God, all become one.

Priel:

Becoming one with the creator, what do they say happens after that deep ecstasy, and how is the state of Baqa coming forth?

Ashoorian:

It is like the Buddhist's Jhana, dying to self, and after that coming back and being present at every breath. And, to always remember yourself in all situations. This will lead to the state of Baqa, a state of extra dimension of being. That inner transformation will lead to the highest state of humanitarianism for serving the public. They believe that a Sufi must always be IN the world, but not OF it.

Priel:

Is the Sufi's main purpose for the poetry, singing and dancing only to attain the state of Fana, or is it also for accomplishing something else?

Ashoorian:

For a Sufi, singing and whirling is not to just immerse and learn knowledge about God, but to learn the actual knowledge of God himself. They wish to lose all the senses of their lower self and experience the ecstasy of surrender, finally attaining Fana.

Priel:

How did the dervishes get the idea to whirl?

Ashoorian:

The whirling is symbolic. In their ceremonies it represents death when performed in black coats, and resurrection when performed in white garb. As legend tells it, the dear and great mystic Sufi master, Shams Tabrizi, had tremendously inspired the poet, Rumi. He was much beloved by Rumi, who dedicated all his collections of poems in his name, "Shams Tabrizi". Shams suffered a horrendous and shocking death. On hearing of it and its circumstances, Rumi began whirling and whirling, singing all of his immortal songs for him. He did this everywhere he went. Beginning from that day on, all of his followers adopted this same pattern.

The circumstances of Shams's death are really interesting. I'll quote something about it from *The Whirling Dervish*, by Shems Friedlander::

"On a Tuesday night in May 1247, Shams Tabrizi left the side of his beloved spiritual brother and stepped into the garden. His killers encircled him and stabbed at his flesh. From the depths of his soul came his cry, "La illaha illa ana" (There is no God but Me), and it was these words uttered with the last breath of Shams that shattered the consciousness of his slayers. When they awoke, all that they found was a few drops of blood, but the body of Shams had disappeared and no trace of it has ever been found."

It is thought that his remark, "There is no God but me," was because he knew that in his dying, he was already becoming one with God.

Priel:

It's my understanding that Sufis believe evil exists, and is a necessary aspect of God. Is that true?

Ashoorian:

I think that is correct. They believe that evil is an adverse energy, a balancing force without which a human will never find his true nature and will always remain a one-dimensional being. Their belief of evil is not something with a tail and horns.

Let me just add a few words about mystic Sufism. All that I have said is just a small portion of their universal philosophy. I also didn't talk about other faculties, like the power of healing, as well as their wonderful psychic and metaphysical abilities.

Priel:

Sufism appears to be a very sweet and benign belief.

Ashoorian:

It truly is.

Priel:

I'd like to bring up the Cabbalists again, your having mentioned them earlier. Would you give some more information about that practice?

Ashoorian:

As I said, the Tree of Life is most likely ancient. Although, Cabbalah developed further, and was most notably practiced in Medieval times. It is a body of mystical teachings arising from rabbinical interpretations of Hebrew scriptures. It stems from oral tradition passed through descendents that God gave Cabbalah to Adam. Basically, it is regarding insight into the nature of God and the soul. Cabbalists believe the world of manifestation is emanation, creation, formation, and action, and beyond that is Ainsoph, from which all existence has come forth.

To some extent, Cabbalistic teachings are secretive and mostly understood only by esoteric scholars. It is thought that every letter, word, and number of the Bible contains mysteries to be interpreted. There is the Cabbalist Gemetria, which used the 22 letters of the Hebrew alphabet and their corresponding numbers to decode hidden meanings in the scriptures, and also to determine a person's character by the numbers in his name.

Numerology is not unique to Cabbalah. Different methods were being used by other people since ancient times. Mesopotamians, Persians, Egyptians, Hindus, and Greeks all had their own kinds of numerology. The Pythagoreans gave certain qualities to individual numbers, and derived meanings from various sums and arrangements.

The method of using numerals has continuously evolved and grown to include more applications, such as using the hour, minute, and date of birth to learn more about a person, and to make predictions. Pythagoras said that evolution is the law of life, number is the law of the universe, and unity is the law of God.

~G o d~

Priel:

Sometimes a philosophy develops among a people that somehow spreads into their religion, or creates their religion. The philosophy can arise from one person's ideas, a small group of elders or leaders, or evolve through the culture of the people. A good part of religions are influenced by politics. That all is understandable. The thing I find amazing, and many people find amusing, is the details religions come up with about their gods.

Ashoorian:

I think you probably mean the many faces, or personalities and actions that have been given about them. Well, as we said, the Babylonians were certainly creative. Their god, Marduk, had 50 faces, or characters. It got a little simpler when people settled down to monotheism.

Priel:

Shelves in bookstores are filled with books written by all kinds of people with all kinds of ideas about what God is. Do you have any idea about the amount of people in the world who still lean towards an image of a god with human-like characteristics?

Ashoorian:

There is still a minority of people believing in a type of god that has human tendencies. For instance, a god that would become angry and make bad things happen, like causing a flood and killing all that he had created.

Whereas, many people, particularly in Eastern countries, believe in a type of god related to elemental forces of nature. Probably, the concept is neither. God is a process of awareness and intelligence in the universe—not a noun or an adjective. It is endless and indescribable. If one day humanity reaches to that type of understanding, then our relationship with God can dramatically change our life. That is because the divine essence of God in us is infinite and indestructible.

If you give the kind of image as human like, you are giving a sense of duality, like black and white, good and bad. The nature of duality is impurity, and God cannot be impure. God would not judge and condemn, but be all understanding and forgiving. I'll give you an example. In one of the Ten Commandments God says, "Do not kill." But in a later chapter in the Old Testament, God says, "Go to Canaan and kill everybody with no exception." This is what I mean by duality.

Priel:

If that might be the way it is, then scriptures which say that God made man in his own image must not mean that God is like a man, but that man has within himself inherent qualities and potentialities that are essences of God. As we all know, Darwinian scientists and followers who believe in biological evolution and natural selection see no place for a god as creator.

Ashoorian:

You and I talked about it earlier. Biological evolution and natural selection are essential and fundamental principles for the physical world to evolve. That was a process to create an archetype, the first perfect pattern from which the entire life of our physical world was copied. Still,

I have to say that all that has happened was eternally in the thought of universal consciousness.

Priel:

I love the remark made by Einstein, "I want to know God's thoughts. Everything else is merely details." But we know that as a scientist, he had the keenest interest in learning details of the universe.

Ashoorian:

Scientists have tried many different ways to reach to a final conclusion, but there are still many doors to open. Matter is made of molecules, which are made of atoms, which consist of electrons and a nuclei. The nuclei's core contains protons and neutrons; beyond protons and neutrons, there are some structureless primordial particles, or elements, which are as yet unexplainable from our scientific point of view.

Ancient wise men in different cultures have named it. Atman, the spirit or soul of the universe, by Hinduism, Universal Consciousness, by Buddhism, and God, Jehovah, Allah and so forth in later religions. Jewish Cabbalists have named it Ainsoph, the ultimate godhood…endless nothingness without any form, yet a "container" of the entire universe. This is put by Rabbi David A Cooper, in his book, *God is a Verb*. The Zohar (Book of Splendor), their most authoritative and original text, states that before form and shape were created, Ainsoph was without form and appearance. Therefore, it is forbidden to perceive it any other way—not even by the letter of the holy name, or by any symbol. Even to perceive what is in the thought of Ainsoph is inconceivable.

The concept of a universal god is that it is timeless in the process of becoming. Not like the way some believe that a god should wind up the clock of the universe or else the world will come to an end. That is not the way the universe works. The universe is continuously perfecting itself. That is the nature of a timeless God. God is a process.

Priel:

Relative to what you've said about God not being a noun, but a verb, an on-going process, I heard a Native American say something very beautiful. He described God as "sacred movement".

Ashoorian:

I love that. Ms. Priel, I'd like to tell you something my son has said to me. Usually, we stay up after midnight talking about everything in the universe, and particularly about the concept of God. One night, when I was talking about cosmic soul and absolute awareness, he said, "Dad, it might not even be that either. I want to tell you about something." This is almost his words:

"I came home from work and lay down on my bed to rest. I became very relaxed, thinking of nothing. Then, I experienced such a vision like I never have in my life. I felt as if I were elevated in a different, pure and innocent realm, like it was prior to time and space. I was in a state of ecstasy. I saw, almost as if I were there, a city of pure crystals and a lake of light. I was soaring, formless, with no identity, no desires, and no boundaries. In that magnificent moment, I was in an ocean of light, in tune and one with all the voices of the sphere. I don't know how long I was in that state dissolved in the bliss." He asked me, "Does this give us a concept of God's realm?"

Priel:

How tremendously vast the concepts in the world are about God! I recently was happy to have the opportunity to attend a performance and have an interview with the fabulous accordion virtuoso, Dick Contino. He happened to mention that he felt a kind of spiritual connection between himself and his audience, and also that same connection with all people.

Later I thought about him and what he had said. Then I began to imagine how he had received his beautiful musical talent, as well the desire to perfect it. I imagined the millions of people who have connected with him while he performed. And, all the people who have played his records and CDs in their homes, connecting with him again and again. From the source where he received that ability, to him, to someone's living room, to where his music might even float through an open window for still others to hear, there is a connection. Like an echo. His performance of *Granada,* will replay in my memory as long as I live.

I thought about Jesus saying the 'Lord's Prayer', and the millions of Christians repeating it through the centuries. How many times are Dr. Martin Luther King's words, "I have a dream," quoted and written about? Those four words echo across our nation. Thomas Edison's invention lights every home in the world. Connection.

How easy it is now, for me to picture the description you give about a divine intelligence which communicates to all that there is throughout all time…the supreme echo of universal magnitude.

Yet, Mr. Ashoorian, despite all that has been said about the magnificence and beauty of God, there is something one has to ask. If there was such power and a plan of such magnitude to create all of this, how can it be that there is so much pain and suffering in life?

Ashoorian:

God doesn't create suffering. We simply should just understand that earth and mankind are perfecting themselves in the evolutionary expansion mode. Some think they have the answer to your question about why is there so much pain and suffering. Some say it is about Karma and reincarnating to a better life, and many Christians believe life is a test for salvation and entrance into heaven.

According to esoteric teachings, like Buddhism, suffering is due to attachment to earthly desires. If one considers life and all that is happening in it as an illusion, not separating himself from the source, as Sufis say, he will live as in the world, not, as being of the world. This is the path that a saint and real spiritual people are living. When one has viewed a saint or spiritual person who has experienced much suffering, it should be understood that to him it is tolerable, that he does not really suffer, because he has mentally removed himself from belonging to the world.

Priel:

That opinion gives the impression that if one removes himself from really living on earth, having no emotions or feelings, things will not be so difficult. It's like that saying of the three monkeys: see no evil, hear no evil, and speak no evil.

Ashoorian:

I hope people will not get that impression. It means that in order to alleviate suffering, you have to live in the world to the fullest, yet not belong to the world by attaching yourself to desires.

Priel:

That philosophy might help psychologically. However, all the agonies of human beings from the beginning of time—natural disasters, hunger, sickness, cruelty—are what turn so many people away from an ability to believe in God or any goodness on earth. Warriors who have mercilessly tortured and annihilated thousands in one day, greed which causes some to steal or deny the very necessities of life from others, neglect or hatred, how can it all be ignored? There has to be a way to resolve that, doesn't there?

Ashoorian:

There are physical laws in the universe which affect our planet, and which are governing the trillions of galaxies throughout space. What happens to our planet at a particular time is just a part of that entire interaction of the universe.

Yet, there are ways to eliminate and solve most of our problems. God has given us all the tools and ability to work on an earth plane as his agent. Let me give you examples. Take the nomads struggling for eons in the deserts of Palestine. Along came others who knew how to make fresh water from the sea, and they turned the desert into a garden paradise. Let us, for a minute, think about recent wars which have cost billions of dollars and destroyed people's lives. Dollars, or tools, were there to instead be spent, along with some really good planning, to give a better life for the people.

From a personal observation, look at my fellow Assyrian people in the north of Iraq, the Cradle of Civilization. After thousands of years under different ethnic regimes, today they are suffering from lack of the essential needs of life despite all the trillions of dollars others make selling oil from our ancestral lands. The tools of profit could be shared properly. On the other hand, there are several million Assyrians through-out the world who, most Sundays, contribute special donations to be sent to those suffering Assyrians in Iraq…using our small tools to help.

Priel:

It's pretty obvious that life on Earth isn't perfect yet. All life on Earth is given the ability to select the best way, and human beings can discern good and bad to make choices.

Ashoorian:

That might be what is considered by some as free will.

Priel:

When I was eleven or twelve, in 1948 or 1949, I was visiting a distant uncle. We were having a quiet chat in his garden when he said to me, "Do you know, there are some people with the preposterous idea that man will go to the moon?" That was something I had never heard before. I thought for a moment, and as if I had always known, I said to him that we would indeed go to the moon and far beyond, learning about the universe, and, more than that, we would learn how to cure and prevent all illness and learn the secret of life itself. That was long before we knew about DNA. I don't know how that idea came to me, but it stayed with me always and I still believe it will be so.

How we can resolve "man's inhumanity to man", I don't know. But mankind is learning so much towards improving physical life through new medical research and by studying about the conditions of our planet and how to cope with them. We are evolving, and using our abilities which were given to us. We can have a better world forever. I personally thank the very few individuals who, with tremendous effort, almost single handedly pursue these endeavors. In a way, they are like avatars of life on Earth. They are the seeds which set the way to bring forth those fruits.

If we would all become more aware, we could speed up the process and contribute, instead of looking up into the North Sky and pleading for help. We really have been given the tools to help ourselves.

Ashoorian:

That, is divine eternal awareness, and you expressed it wonderfully.

~Auras and Souls~

Priel:

Lots of people think we are surrounded by spirits, energies, and people's souls. Cultures in all times across the earth claimed to have supernatural experiences. For mankind, anything one cannot explain seems mystical. Anything unknown seems powerful. It was mystical for ancient man that there was night and day…light and dark. Now that we know what causes it, that the earth revolves around the sun, the mystical aspect is resolved.

Ashoorian:

The universe swarms with things we don't understand.

Priel:

On the first page of this book you began speaking of a creative and silent communication of infinite wisdom sending thought, memory, and purpose throughout the universe. Every section of the book echoes that same strain…God communicating the plan to the universe and to life on earth, the communication of germs and all living things to multiply and evolve, shamans gaining knowledge, divine ability, and inspiration. People communicate thoughts to others, and sometimes know something before it happens. Some people think spirits communicate with them. Is it possible all of that communication is another kind of energy which travels through some type of waves in space? Can it be that they are particle impulses, which come from the same type of source? I'm not expecting that anyone could have these answers.

Ashoorian:

Since you didn't expect perfect answers to your remarks, I'll gladly comment on some of them. Unfortunately, most of the world's wonderful libraries of ancient times were destroyed by conquerors, with tremendous loss of the old scientists' writings about their methods and research. You mention that everything might come from the same type of source. I would say, yes, and that it is the living fire emanating from that highest, supreme eternal soul which permeates the entire universe and runs the engine of every phenomenon of the visible and invisible realm.

People from long ago wrote about halos—auras or energy fields —surrounding human bodies. It's a wide-held belief that people have energies surrounding them, but little has been proven about what exactly it is. Everyone is familiar with the Renaissance paintings depicting halos around saints, Jesus Christ, and Saint Mary. The idea for that might have come from the Bible, which talks about a light surrounding angels, Jesus, and others.

Decades ago, Semyon Kirlian, a Russian electrician, discovered a process thought to photograph this energy field around people. He produced photos that showed humans with an aura glowing from their body in different colored layers. He thought it was the soul. Later on, scientists experimented on the energy field, or aura, of plants. One of the experiments which was the most discussed of their findings was that they cut a leaf in half, and using the Kirlian process took a photo of the part of the leaf still remaining on the plant. The photographic result showed a matrix aura still remaining around the place of the missing part of the leaf.

For certain, scientists know humans do radiate some energy which can be measured. There is electromagnetism from our nervous system, which is detected with Galvano meters. Sonograms pick up sonic vibrations from our body such as heartbeats, breath, etc. Heat radiating from our body can be measured with infrared cameras. Other energies which might be there have not been put to the test by scientific devices as yet.

Priel:

Anyone might wonder what goes on in those various energy levels as they are surrounding the body. And, more so, what undetected energy levels might be there. Complex ideas have been written about auras. Why don't you give a brief summary of the history and of what is currently considered about auras?

Ashoorian:

Throughout history the idea of a universal energy of all the matter in nature has been argued by different great masters, such as Pythagoras, in the sixth century B.C. It was believed that this energy can cause an interaction between two individuals at a distance, and has a variety of effects on the human organism, including the cure of illnesses.

In ancient countries, like India, the great sages spoke about a sort of universal energy called Prana, or some called it the breath of life. In China, their great masters knew about such a vital energy around all living creatures, which was called Chi. Even in Cabbalah, Jewish mystics would refer to such an energy and call it Astral light. This type of energy was observed by many scientists in the eighteenth and nineteenth centuries. In particular, Count Wilhelm von Reichenback spent thirty years of his life experimenting on this energy field which he called Odice Force. It is a common subject that Egyptians and Tibetans completely understood the technique of the power of mind over matter, and were able to manifest the spirit force over astral and physical substances to bring forth some entities to be attached to their tombs and guard them for centuries.

It has been said that cosmic energy is composed of negative and positive energies, so the human energy is manifested through the same composition. Some researchers have described the human energy field, commonly called auras, in seven layers. The physical body consists of liquids, solids, and gases, and are the first three layers. Beyond that are the four etheric layers, which are ether, astral, mental, and spiritual, and are thought to be associated with extrasensory communication capabilities, cosmic knowledge, enhanced creativity, and spiritual connections, the last of which is limitless. When these frequency layers are in balance, a person is able to conceive positive thought forms, be more aware, receptive, and intuitive, and to influence his own healing.

Priel:

It seems a profusion of material has become attached to the subject of auras. It's intriguing to think that someday scientists might learn more about our energies, and how some paranormal things actually exist. I know you will be telling about topics relative to that later on. When one listens to descriptions of auras, it's easy to imagine how paranormal phenomena might happen.

In the field of Science there is such a polarity in the view of science's function and use. Some see it as the perfect, exact way to know the universe, and wish to remain only with the structured information they have studied. Others, on the opposite side, view science as a brilliant tool to investigate and search new concepts and visions. Brave scientists, like Einstein, search and dream far beyond. With the large percentage of things not understood, why can so many scientists remain comfortable and secure with only what they know has been proven?

They have a limited view that if they don't know the answer to something, it doesn't exist.

Ashoorian:

In their scientific world, western countries view the whole universe as a material object made of substances. Eastern philosophies have a different idea. They believe that the material universe is notrooted in matter, but in an invisible, pure consciousness from which the whole material of the universe has been emanated. It would be difficult for the scientists to step out of the standard structure of their studies and, like Einstein, to search and dream beyond the physical world. With that narrow perception, an invisible realm cannot pass through their mind at all.

However, regarding psychical phenomena, there are good signs that some modern scientists are coming to a common ground with those who believe in an invisible realm. According to *Time Books*, of Time, Inc., at Princeton University, Professor Robert Jahn has been the head of the Princeton Engineering Anomalies Research laboratory for more than two decades. He says that for years they have been finding data that conventional science doesn't have the tools to deal with, and that the mainstream scientists don't know what to do with it so they ignore it. Another scientist involved with anomalous methods of communication, Professor Daryl Bem, from Cornell University, agrees.

There are some more good people researching the subject, including the Stanford Research Institute. I have a lot of hope that the time will come for the human race to interact in a mystical and ethereal level with the invisible realm. But for the time being, everything not understood is still alien to many.

Priel:

A smart man tries to memorize information. But a brilliant man tries to analyze and understand a bigger picture…to see the whole forest and not just many individual trees. Since there have been countless supernatural occurrences throughout history, it seems strange that scientists don't wonder more about the existence of at least some of it and have the desire to investigate more.

Ashoorian:

Many people are under the impression that the invisible realm is a demonic realm which should be excluded from their life. Even talking about it is blasphemy. As I said earlier, even some of the modern scientists who are trapped in a limited frame will not let the appearance of the invisible realm become conventional belief.

Priel:

Do some people consider auras to be souls?

Ashoorian:

That is where people are confused. Auras and souls are not the same thing at all. A soul is entirely different.

Priel:

Souls are an important concept of various religions. When we talk about a connection with God, it seems like Eastern beliefs, and also those of olden American Indians, consider themselves as being a part of God with all of the nature of the universe. Whereas, much of Western religion views just a portion of themselves connecting with God by means of a soul.

There has been a terrible worry about souls throughout the centuries, with wars being fought regarding the concern that one's beliefs and conduct would determine where one's soul might end up after death. Probably the two major sources of conjectures about souls stem from Hindu and Christian religions.

Ashoorian:

Most Christians believe that a soul goes to heaven, purgatory, or even Hell, after physical death, making that soul personal to only that particular human being. Hindus believe that a soul returns to earth repeatedly to enter many different material bodies, the soul being an entity of its own—reincarnating. In the Old Testament there are passages where Hebrews speak about certain individuals returning to earth again in the body of another person. Some Indians of the Americas believed their own soul came from, and returned to, a special place.

Priel:

In recent years, New Age devotees of metaphysics and spirituality have been prolific theorizers and writers about souls. A good number of them think souls reincarnate. Also, some people think ghosts are synonymous with the energy of a soul. What is a soul, if there is one? I've heard about souls within our body, souls in the sky, souls in heaven, old souls, etc. Where and when do you think the first idea of a soul came to be, and what are the many views of what it is?

Ashoorian:

The subject of the soul is so complicated that words fail to give real definition about it, because it is beyond human experiences. Generally, it is believed that the source of all souls is the universal soul from which all other souls are a part and an aspect.

Frenchman, Allan Kardec, the esteemed author, scholar, and instructor of the Sciences, became intrigued with the number of strange phenomena related to the nature of spirits. He decided to use his skills in solid scientific background to research the subject. Most noteworthy, hundreds of people throughout the world contacted him with their experiences. He asked many things of those whom he considered acceptable people with valid experiences or investigations in the subject.

Selecting responses with the majority of similarities, he collected them in a book, *The Spirits Book*, published in 1857. From then until today, most people who study and write about spiritism derive their information and opinions from that source.

From early times, human beings felt that personal desires and actions are functioning through a mysterious and unknown power in their life. Millennia after that, particularly in India, that power was called Atman. Atman to Indian people meant Universal Soul. Native Americans called it the Great Spirit. To some westerners it was considered as electromagnetic force, a mysterious soul with everything we sense and desire functioning through that form.

Cabbalah describes the soul as a magnetic field without any boundary. Cabbalists believe the human physical body is formed from the combination of four elements, but that the soul is formed from four combinations of wind which has some unknown principles.

In the *Bhagavad-Gita,* it is written about the soul that fire cannot burn it, water cannot make it wet, wind cannot blow it away, and sword cannot cut it in two. This was the belief of ancient sages who stated that we must have something intangible which we were born in. We are told that when a person is born, the Atman gives a part of itself to the physical body, and it is called Jiva. That spiritual part is like a drop of water taken from an eternal vast ocean which has all the quality of the original cosmic soul and is a part of all that exists.

Other sages of old times, and some of modern times, have claimed that souls have had a process through the four different kingdoms. The first is the kingdom of minerals, the second one is the kingdom of vegetation, the third is the kingdom of animals, and finally the last one is human kingdom. This has been stated as a principal of evolution for the soul to journey through the physical realm.

Priel:

All you are saying describes a kind of one divine and all encompassing soul of the universe. But what about all the people who think they have their own personal soul which they carry with them to heaven, or whatever else happens with it?

Ashoorian:

The human soul is a portion of that universal soul which is the infinite and indestructible essence of God. It is beyond all the materialistic form of life. To realize and approach such a brilliant state of understanding, we need to learn and believe in that divine and infinite source from which our own souls came to existence. As I said, human soul alchemically was transmuted from base through four different kingdoms to an absolute intelligent soul, uniting with that soul of God.

Priel:

From the way you paint it, I imagine in my mind that individual souls are like little atoms making up one whole soul of the universe.

Ashoorian:

What a beautiful analogy. I believe in that, and in addition, I believe that if we learn the purpose and language of our soul, and arrive in touch with the connection between our awareness and soul, we will be taken to a much greater level of hierarchy which will benefit the entire physical realm of the human race.

These high frequencies are assisting us in our lower realm, although we are not aware of it. It is happening at a different level of human soul which is connected to that part of universal hierarchy. All of these might be a portion of reality about that cosmic consciousness that we are analyzing and describing with our earthly standards. As Deepak

Chopra put it in his book, *How to Know God*, "The soul is as mysterious as God, and we have just a few reliable facts about it."

Priel:

If souls are a part of God, or the goodness of the universe, shouldn't they then be perfect?

Ashoorian:

A soul in the spirit realm is pure and innocent, with no duality, and is not subjected to any earthly condition. The instant it splits itself to interact in the physical level, a specific personality is created to accomplish the desired tendencies of that lifetime.

Priel:

Knowing what we do about DNA, genes, and so forth, it seems more like the personality would form first, and distort a pure soul which is drawn into it.

Ashoorian:

It is supposed that a soul, prior to its reincarnating, has in mind the pattern of the personality to accomplish its desire. We can talk more about this soon.

Priel:

Would humans be responsible, or expected, to maintain the purity of the soul, if that is possible with all of our moral and human frailties?

Ashoorian:

We are responsible for the purity of our soul. That part of our spirit which interacts with our emotions and other earthly problems is responsible not to create a bad karma. Otherwise, it will have to work hard in this lifetime or the next to compensate. The other portion of our soul, which is related to Universal Soul, will remain pure and under no circumstances could be affected. Again, I will come up with a sentence from Deepak Chopra. He says, " The soul of a saint and the soul of a criminal at the end of their life remain pure and innocent."

Priel:

Based upon what you've described about souls thus far, what happens to a soul after a person dies?

Ashoorian:

If we believe that we are a part of that universal soul which is infinite and without beginning and end, we have to believe that we never die. We just are in process through different phases and dimensions for an unknown and mysterious reason, which some say is for learning lessons in each lifetime we take.

Priel:

What happens to a soul when it has completed its goal and has accomplished the entire process of its karma?

Ashoorian:

At that stage, the soul will reenter the highest level of the spirit realm. Those purified souls who have attained that level of purification have no longer to be reborn and experience again the suffering of earthly life. Unless, the cosmic soul or God wants them to reincarnate in a perfect body with a divine essence to help the human race, like all the great prophets of the world.

Priel:

What about those souls who have not accomplished their goals and have not yet been purified?

Ashoorian:

Those souls will stay in a particular level in the spirit realm according to the degree of their purification, in order to evolve and elevate themselves for the next reincarnation.

Priel:

Reincarnation is a subject which has not been accepted by many people, and in particular churches' authorities.

Ashoorian:

There are millions who believe in reincarnation, and have some ideas about it. Nevertheless, you are correct that churches' authorities will not accept it. There are many cases in the Old and New Testaments that obviously talk about reincarnation, and especially the Book of Mathew, Chapter 17, Lines 10 to 12. However, it has been stated by many scholars that in the year A.D. 533, under the Emperor Justinian, the Catholic church ordered all teachings of reincarnation removed from the scriptures. Instead, they emphasized the subject of Paradise and Hell, the day of judgment and punishment, plus a god to be feared. Therefore, it cannot be expected that churches will confirm the subject of reincarnation.

Priel:

Can a soul communicate with loved ones after death of its body?

Ashoorian:

I think all of us have experienced a communication with loved ones who are in the spirit realm, either through our dreams or in an altered state of meditation. We human beings have different degrees of consciousness. Those who are in a higher level are more capable to receive communication with their loved ones.

Priel:

Some declare that there are old and new souls. How can a soul which has no material body be old or new?

Ashoorian:

Not literally old or new. That is due to the different degree of the soul's purification. Basically, it is believed that old souls have gone through many lifetimes on the earth, and are in a higher degree of awareness. Whereas, new souls are those who have recently been reincarnated in the human kingdom and their awareness is in a lower degree.

Priel:

How does a soul retain a bad karma? Does it happen in a mind level of the soul to remember the wrong things it has done in its lifetime?

Ashoorian:

We've been told that the soul retains its memories in mind level from previous lifetimes and has a purpose in mind before reincarnating. The purpose is to create a personality to interact and accomplish in that specific lifetime. So, if that individual personality did not accomplish the purpose of the soul, a great imbalance will be created between the soul and personality. That is what is called karma, the universal law of cause and effect. For this very reason, if that personality could not balance that bad karma in this lifetime, the soul will create another personality to purify the bad karma in a next lifetime. No living beings can escape the golden law of karma, or cause and effect, which is not subjected to change under any circumstances. We receive whatever we give.

Priel:

That sounds like they are saying a soul thinks and has a kind of emotion.

Ashoorian:

Probably, but their emotions and desires are not like ours. Their intention is to manifest themselves in the physical world for the purpose of purification and reaching a hierarchy level, in order to be out of the birth and death cycle.

Priel:

If a soul creates a personality in order to make a better balance in that particular lifetime, what causes an imbalance between itself and the personality?

Ashoorian:

That particular personality might start interacting in a very wild and evil way. If this happens, the soul might detach itself from that person and leave him to act and live his life the way he wants until his life comes to an end.

Priel:

What is the difference between a soul and a prespirit?

Ashoorian:

The prespirit is formed from a sort of substances which appears as vapor, semi material. Its origin is from a kind of fluid in the atmosphere of our globe. In other words, from the four elements of the earth. The soul, which is surrounded by prespirit, is the real universal soul, which comes directly from God and is the essence of our life.

Priel:

Earlier you said that a soul retains its memories. How can that happen, since it no longer has its material body?

Ashoorian:

After the death of material body, the soul absorbs a sort of substances from the atmosphere of the concerning planet which was represented by its prespirit in its last life time. That atmospheric fluid enables the soul to retain its memories.

Priel:

Would the soul hover in a particular layer around the earth?

Ashoorian:

That part of our spirit which is formed from atmospheric substances and is called prespirit does, in some particular situations, hover all around the different places. It is believed that when a person is killed instantly in an accident, the prespirit will be confused and left behind in a lost state, because it was not expecting that sudden death.

After wandering for a period of time, eventually it will be absorbed into those elements from which it came. Most of the haunted places are occupied by such left behind prespirits desperately hovering around, because they can not overcome their death and cross the earth's boundaries to become one with the absolute universal soul.

Priel:

Do the spirits communicate with each other in the spirit realm?

Ashoorian:

It has been said that all the spirits do communicate with each other in their spirit world, especially with regard to learning and teaching. Spirit guides, in particular. There are two kinds of spirit guides. One kind has never experienced a physical life. It is more aligned with the goodness in the universe. The other kind might be deceased masters, or sometimes ancestors of the recipient. If a spirit guide has no expertise in a particular field to guide his partner on the other side, it will communicate with another spirit which has expertise in that concerning field for the essential help. Mostly, spirits communicate with each other for learning the eternal wisdom of their realm.

Priel:

I have to say, that by now my head is spinning. Is it awareness of our soul, or DNA of our body, which has the secret of our evolution?

Ashoorian:

As I said earlier, our awareness is a flowing stream from cosmic soul through which our existing evolution has been guided; therefore, our soul's awareness contained the seed of evolution. Our DNA and nerve system are functioning according to the order and pattern given to their molecules before the helix of DNA was formed.

Priel:

Tell us more about those souls that have never experienced physical life on the earth.

Ashoorian:

This type of being is from a different realm with a different consciousness not to be described with our earthly vocabulary and human terms. There might be many other forms of life in millions of galaxies which might have solar systems like ours, but in a different dimension. I would say a dimension, for instance, like an angelic kingdom with different frequencies and qualities of consciousness.

Priel:

Should it be supposed that those beings cause a karma like is presumed on earth?

Ashoorian:

Cause and effect apply to all living beings in our physical world. This is a universal law. Karma cannot be attributed to those kinds of nonphysical beings, because their world and kingdom have no boundaries, and are beyond time and space.

Priel:

Here is my final question about the soul. Many pet lovers like to think that their animals have souls. What about animals having a soul like human beings?

Ashoorian:

I think I will quote some lines from scientist, Gary Zukav, the award winning author of, *The Dancing Wuli Master*. In his following book entitled, *The Seat of the Soul*, he put it this way:

> "Each human being has a soul. The journey toward individualsoulhood is what distinguishes the human kingdom from the animal kingdom and the mineral kingdom. Only the human kingdom has the experience of individual soulhood. That is why its powers of creation are great.
>
> The soul process moved through degrees of awareness. Animals, for example, do not have individual soul. They have group soul. Each animal is a part of a group soul…
>
> Consider, for example, the group soul of buffalo. There is one group soul of enormous impersonal energy that is called, buffalo.It is an enormous expansive sphere of impersonal energy that is buffalo consciousness, it exists at a level of simply energy

dynamics, not individual selfhood. That energy is in continual movement…

…Instinctual behavior is the way of the group soul."

Priel:

Using imagination, I can kind of see what he might have in mind when I picture colonies of ants and bees. For the subject of souls in general, one can't help but compare the way the world has come up with so many intricate details about souls, to the way the world has come up with the many actions, purposes, and rules about God and religions. Those ideas of such an intriguingly complex soul life might seem to be that well-intended and good persons may have gone too far in their assumptions and interpretations.

Communication

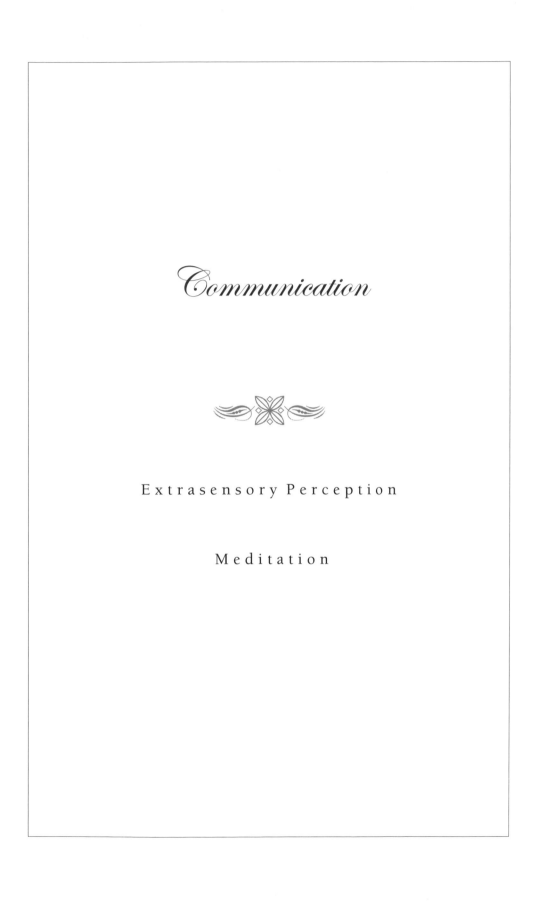

Extrasensory Perception

Meditation

~Extrasensory Perception~

Priel:

Tales of seas parting, healing with mind and hands, psychic predictions...? From the first idea of creation, to today's New Age theories, people have thought there might be spiritual or unknown phenomena occurring. All humanity has been influenced or tantalized by it. Even nations. Many phenomena have collectively come to be placed into the synonymous titles of Supernatural, Paranormal, or Metaphysical.

First, can we talk about the non-verbal receiving of information some people experience? Today it is moderately accepted that some of it is valid. The means by which it is received varies. Knowing about something which is happening somewhere else, knowing about something which will happen later, exchanging thoughts between two individuals, the power of the mind and thought forms—is there some scientific information which can explain to what this phenomenon might be attributed?

Ashoorian:

Well, I'll try to describe an experiment which was performed by some physicists. They split a subatomic particle into two pieces, and placed the spinning pieces apart from one another. They changed the direction of the spin on one of them, and the other piece instantaneously changed its spin to correspond with that of its twin. They found out that the spin changing was faster than the speed of light. It means no time was consumed for this change no matter the distance. This is the way we interact and get information and thought forms from each other in human frequency. This proves that we all are part of the whole. The universe is emanated from consciousness, not matter. Therefore, consciousness does not need time to fill a gap between two objects.

Priel:

Hundreds, probably thousands, of books have been written in recent years relating to all the metaphysical subjects. I remember several decades ago there was excitement among New Age devotes, as well as religious persons, who were pursuing information about paranormal phenomena. For some, it was for fun. Some were looking to quickly acquire psychic skills, or to gain advice from beyond our physical realm. For others it is a serious belief that stems from teachings of masters from antiquity. What happened with all those who were so keen?

Ashoorian:

Unfortunately, the fever for this phenomenon declined very fast, and those who were curious and expected to become a master in this field vanished from all seminars and other spiritual gatherings after a short time. To me, it was very obvious that would happen. Once a Sufi told me, "Spirituality cannot be learned, and it will not come from outside of us. If you do not have faith to understand that, do not waste your time." After fifty years, I am still searching. But I never gave up, because I reached to a point in my life where I understood that spirituality is a hidden elixir which needs a lifetime to even scratch the surface of its phenomenon.

Priel:

Are the various ways communication occurs merely subtle differences in the same thing, and all considered as psychic experience?

Ashoorian:

This is a very good question. First of all, the word psychic probably does not suit this natural gift which is our birth right. The ability we have in extrasensory perception and other facets similar to that should not be considered supernatural, because every bit of it is pure natural.

However, if you would ask me who is psychic, I will say a psychic person either instantaneously receives, or is capable to bring forth through divination or a natural way, some information from beyond our physical realm. It is termed Extrasensory Perception, commonly called ESP. It means going beyond our five senses and perceiving an extra sense of information beyond time and space. ESP has come to be categorized in different facets, such as clairvoyance, clairaudience, precognition, premonition, telepathy, psychometry, psychokinesis, and so on.

Priel:

What actually happens in clairvoyance?

Ashoorian:

A clairvoyant person can be in a different area and describe from a distance details about something of which he has no prior knowledge. He has the ability to see or feel an object or subject unseen by him previously in his physical world. In other words, to perceive information beyond our five senses.

Priel:

I recall when NASA was sending their Voyager to Jupiter. Several leading psychics were brought to meditate about what would be seen on the surface of the planet. What the psychics came up with individually was all the same thing. Years later, when information came back from the Voyager, it was the same as what the psychics had seen. Moreover, the psychics had given greater details.

Ashoorian:

I remember that. The gifted psychic, Ingo Swann, termed that kind of ability, "remote viewing". He was one of those psychics you just mentioned. At that time, he said that there were rings around Jupiter. Scientists thought that was ridiculous. Of course, Mr. Swann was vindicated when the Voyager confirmed Jupiter did indeed have rings. In the 1970s, he was engaged for certain psychic studies by the Stanford Research Institute. During that same period, the United States Defense Agency and the CIA were wishing for reliable psychic techniques for intelligence purposes. While the Cold War was going on, the Soviets were spending large amounts on psychic research. They wanted to use psychic ability to spy from a distance on secret documents. "Remote viewers" for the United States have helped locate missiles, projects for biological warfare, and underground installations.

Priel:

I'd like to ask you a question about voices. Some people say a voice tells them things, rather than their feeling it or seeing it.

Ashoorian:

This type of experience is clairaudience. Clairaudients are people who hear voices which give advice and information. Some experts call it an inner voice coming from our higher self. Others say it is a voice from our spirit guide which comes from the other side. All this is working and happening by a superior law we cannot comprehend. Many great musicians, for instance Bach, Beethoven, and, particularly, Mozart, are thought to have received some of their masterpieces from the music of the sphere. On his deathbed, Mozart dictated the completion of his *Requiem* to a master musician at such speed that the master could hardly keep up. When it was finished, there was not one note incorrectly dictated. For this reason, many scholars consider Mozart might have been a clairaudient.

Priel:

Not long ago, I watched a documentary about the composer and conductor, Leonard Bernstein. He occasionally would arrive at a very difficult point when writing a composition, and struggle with it for a long time. Eventually, he would give up and go lie down for a few hours. Suddenly, he would jump up with all the music coming to him solved.

I remember your telling me that your lyrics come to you suddenly. Even those you and your people consider to be your masterpieces. I, myself, have witnessed you composing, on two separate occasions, very dramatic poems in a matter of a few minutes. There is no doubt that you and the afore mentioned people were given very rare talents in your respective fields, and also have possessed great emotional passion for the subjects. However, you have told me that you feel you receive assistance.

Ashoorian:

Well, as far as Mr. Bernstein is concerned, I don't have any information as to how he experienced things. Deep relaxation, even some meditation, helps free the mind from the debris of unnecessary and unwanted thoughts. A significant amount does come to me in the night, but it also comes suddenly at other times. Sometimes my own inner voice dictates to me, and at other times I actually hear a voice. It comes so fast that it is difficult to get it all written down, or to even remember it all. Often I agonize that I'm not making it as good as what I originally heard. Perhaps talent and words were given to me for a purpose. For this reason, I have never accepted royalties for any of the recorded albums using my lyrics. I prefer to donate the income to help my Assyrian people struggling in Iraq.

Priel:

The most well-known phenomenon in ESP is telepathy.

Ashoorian:

Basically, telepathy has been considered mind communication between two individuals. Thoughts are transferred from a person who is the sender, to another person who is the receiver, simultaneously bringing the subject to a conscious level. A strong desire between sender and receiver is the first important factor for the success of telepathic communication. Telepathy is spontaneous, and can also be induced and premeditated in advance.

Priel:

The most common phenomenon occurring with psychics and sensitives is precognition. It also appears to be of the greatest interest or curiosity for most people.

Ashoorian:

Most precognitive experiences are happening spontaneously. I personally get an odd feeling about something that I am not aware is going to happen. Then, suddenly, a strong impression about the subject crosses my mind for a few seconds. After a short period of time, that event happens almost exactly the way that I have felt it was going to be. This phenomenon still astounds me.

I know there is a universal law for all that is happening with the different types of psychic experiences categorized. ESP, sixth sense, or some other sense of higher self beyond all this, might not be accurate definitions for this phenomenon.

Priel:

What is the category where a person gets a feeling about an event, but can't define precisely what is going to happen?

Ashoorian:

That might be called premonition. It is a milder form of precognition. One might get a feeling of an event, but be unable to define the actual scene of the event.

Priel:

A person might be walking through a new area and get the feeling he somehow has been there before. Or, he may be doing something not normally done by him, and get the sense that he had done exactly the same thing at some time in the past. That has been termed De ja vu. Is it, actually, that he has had a precognition in the past and it is long forgotten?

Ashoorian:

Exactly, that is what is believed. Of course, some have an idea about it that it might be a spontaneous regression reminding them of something in the past. However, in my opinion, we can consider it as precognition.

Priel:

Psychometry has been described as a capability to derive an impression about an event or a person from the past.

Ashoorian:

A psychometrist will claim to see and interpret an emotional event having occurred prior to the present time, but which is still remaining in the etheric level. A person who is experienced in this, by touching an object which was in the immediate time of an event, or an object which belonged to a person, will replay the event in a different way. He is not actually reconstructing the event itself, but he is developing an imprint of the event through his etheric level.

Priel:

That sounds like there would be a kind of matrix of the energy created while the event was occurring.

Ashoorian:

Some experiments have been done by famous mediums who have been taken to historical places where important and unsolved events have been happening. They have come up with details about the event which may have happened hundreds of years before.

Priel:

What about hypnosis? Is hypnosis the mind power of a strong person willing a weaker person to perform in a particular way, or is it something else?

Ashoorian:

It is not mind control. Hypnosis is a process that leads a person into a deeply relaxed state where the conscious mind is reduced and the subconscious is entered. The brain waves are like in a sleep or dream stage. Medical studies are learning more about the way the brain's cerebral cortex is affected during hypnisis. Hypnosis has been proven useful in helping to block pain, and in some behavioral therapy.

Priel:

A category under ESP which is different from the others is psychokinesis. It has been considered as a fantasy, particularly in Hollywood movies like Superman and films in which characters do extraordinary physical things impossible in our physical world. What definition is available to describe psychokinesis?

Ashoorian:

Most people have heard the true story about the little girl who lifted an automobile which had fallen on her father as he was changing a tire. Psychokinesis is an ability to affect physical matter by perhaps moving an object, or bending something, for instance metal, without using physical means. A psychokinesist will focus through his focal center, that area between his eyebrows called the third eye in metaphysical terms, onto an object and change its state or move it.

Priel:

Is psychokinesis considered to be the power of the mind over matter?

Ashoorian:

In fact, many researchers have stated that the true source of this ability is not power of mind, but consider it to be a strong non-physical energy that we all possess. Whatever way it is accomplished, either the power of mind over matter, or non-physical energy, doesn't matter. What does matter is that this mysterious phenomenon appears to work.

Priel:

Quite a few books suggest that some ancient monoliths and structures were erected in this manner of psychokinesis. How do they think that could have happened?

Ashoorian:

There are huge erections all over the world for which such construction could not have been done by any means we know about. Some believe even the great pyramids of Egypt might have been erected by the art of levitation. Or, in other words, by the power of phychokinesis. Edgar Cayce, of America, explained from one of his readings how a high priest learned the art of levitation in Atlantis 9,500 years ago, and returned to Egypt and built the Great Pyramids with the help of other high priests. This art has been used in modern times as well. Many experiments have been performed and documented by some experts and researchers.

Priel:

What kinds of experiments? Can you be specific?

Ashoorian:

Yes, of course. A well-known experiment was performed in this way. They placed a metallic object like a key or spoon on a table in front of a psychokinesist and asked him to demonstrate this art. The psychokinesist began concentrating in order to collect his energy. After a short period of time, he focused through his focal center, or third eye, and allowed the energy to flow toward a specific spot on that metal object. Then continuously, with great intention, he bombarded that specific area to disintegrate the atomic elements of it and change the rate of its vibration. After some time, the object was bent at the same spot on which he had focused.

Priel:

You said earlier that psychokinesis is an art. How is that reconciled with being an extrasensory phenonmenon?

Ashoorian:

This particular paranormal activity is not so much about receiving information. It is more about that same energy beyond our physical realm through which we can concentrate and direct vibrations of the elements required to bring about the results.

Priel:

What about moving and elevating objects? How could that happen?

Ashoorian:

It has been suggested that by the power of their mind and concentration the masters were able to create a vacuum around objects and eliminate the earth's gravity, like lifting huge blocks of stone. It might be as Edgar Cayce said about the great pyramid. It is so easy for people to believe the reports from his readings, because he has been correct such a large percentage of times.

I should step away from ESP for a moment and mention the Free Masons, who were masters of the stone laying trade that also later developed into being a service and spiritual society. They were responsible for the building of many colossal cathedrals, and some suggest they originated in Egypt and were involved in building the Great Pyramids. Marvelous engineering feats of the past are coming to light in recent years.

Priel:

Maybe that priest who went to Atlantis brought back engineering techniques for lifting stones! Anyway, there is something else I have been wondering about regarding ESP. There is the experience when someone gains knowledge or insight, rather than experiencing a vision of a particular event occurring. Could that be considered a prophesy?

Ashoorian:

Not a prophesy, however it might be from collective unconscious, which we talked about much earlier.

Priel:

As mentioned earlier, collective unconscious is the idea of Carl Jung, the famous psychoanalyst of the twentieth century. What is a good definition of collective unconscious? Can you give more information about it?

Ashoorian:

Carl Jung believed that an energy source is stored somewhere in a sphere which contains all the memories and knowledge of the entire human race. Those individual souls who are able to tune in to that bank of memories will get the knowledge and any other information they desire. He termed it as collective unconscious.

Priel:

Going back to visions just a bit, skeptics say that visions are probably hallucinations, or even imaginings of unstable persons. Yet, mentally rational people see things. A good example, is astronaut Buzz Aldrin. Our astronauts are put through rigorous testing of psychological, rational, and logical abilities. They are exceptionally intelligent and well educated, as well. Mr. Aldrin and other astronauts say they have seen UFOs when they were in outer space. We have to accept that those credible men saw something. Therefore, would reasoning be the same that rational people could experience symbolic visions?

Ashoorian:

Symbolic visions are like symbolic dreams. There is a universal language to interpret the symbols of visions or dreams which are trying to tell us something. About Mr. Aldrin, it is hard to say that what he saw was a symbolic vision or a real UFO. His experience depends on the details of what he saw.

Priel:

Pausing temporarily from ESP, and speaking of UFOs, what should we think about them?

Ashoorian:

UFOs have been a great puzzle all over the world in the last half of the twentieth century. The rash of unexplained sightings have been the subject of speculation for millions of people in different countries. I, personally, just for the sake of curiosity have been following this case more than half of my life, but unfortunately have reached nowhere. Of course, recently the subject is not so hot as it was two decades ago. Nobody knows why there is a complete silence, or in another words, a hush up among the authorities of the air force in the United States.

UFOs have been verified by many famous people, including scientists and scholars. Even President Harry Truman, president of the United States, in a press conference in 1955, declared, "I assure you that UFOs exist, and it is not constructed by any power on the earth." President Jimmy Carter experienced a UFO sighting while in office.

In the Old Testament there are many subjects regarding some kind of flying objects. The most profound and significant is regarding Ezekiel, the high priest of the Hebrew nation, when he was in captivity in Babylon by the river Chebar. In the first chapter of the Book of Ezekiel, he has explained how he saw something like flying objects which he took to be living beings. We must consider how a man from ancient times, before there were machines and lights, might think. I'll quote some highlights:

Verse 4: "I looked, behold, a stormy wind came out of the north, and a great cloud, with brightness round about it, and fire flashing forth continually, and in the midst of the fire, as it were gleaming bronze.

Verse 15-19: Now as I looked at the living creatures, I saw a wheel upon the earth beside the living creatures, one for each of the four of them. As for the appearance of the wheels and their construction: their appearance was like the gleaming of chrysolite; and the four had the same likeness, their construction being as it were a wheel within a wheel. When they went, they went in any of their four directions without turning as they went. The four wheels had rims and they had spokes; and their rims were full of eyes round about. And when the living creatures went, the wheels went beside them; and when the living creatures rose from the earth, the wheels rose.

Verse 24: And when they went, I heard the sound of their wings like the sound of many waters, like the thunder of the Almighty,…"

Of course, there were other things written which I didn't mention, but some scholars have erected a great monument according to what Ezekiel has described in those above passages. This monument has been placed on the grounds of an American university, and under it there is a plaque which says, "The wheel inside the wheel of Ezekiel". So with all the above in mind, what do you expect me to say? Am I supposed to believe in UFO phenomena, or not!

Priel:

In the sixteenth century there were reports by many citizens in Nuremburg, Germany, that they saw disks and spheres in the sky. A few years later, people in Basel, Switzerland observed similar flying objects overhead. If there is such a thing, one could suppose they have been coming and going for perhaps hundreds or thousands of years. There wouldn't have been any cameras, newspapers, or television to tell about it at those times. And the world was only sparsely populated and in scattered places, so word of mouth wouldn't spread many tales. Therefore, when it is said UFOs are a recent happening, that might be incorrect. Another point to be considered is time. Years for us might be only minutes for another. That is, if there is such a thing.

Ashoorian:

Those are quite interesting thoughts.

Priel:

Returning now to our metaphysical discussion, unfortunately there have been fraudulent people making all kinds of claims about their abilities for money or fame. But some inexplicable things occurred in my youth and adulthood which have caused wonderment for me.

I always have attempted to rationalize very simple reasons for them, but a few too many have happened for me to just let them pass. That has lead to many long talks with you regarding information you have acquired, and ultimately has lead to these writings you and I are now doing.

Ashoorian:

As I mentioned earlier, extrasensory phenomena are everybody's birth right, but those who are afraid to break the boundaries of their beliefs, and who ignore any kind of phenomena beyond their five senses, have difficulty comprehending and responding to these experiences. From the beginning, I knew that you had a strong feeling that there was more than just the material world. Yet, I also began calling you Doubting Thomas.

Priel:

I wish I could describe to you a few incidents which have happened to me, and see how you explain, or define them.

Ashoorian:

We can do that.

Priel:

It's embarrassing to speak personally, because I know, as do other people who keep such things to themselves, that we open ourselves to ridicule. However, I can tell you about one for which I have a living witness.

One time when I was fifty, it was Spring, and I was enjoying an auto trip through the wine country with a friend. As we drove peacefully down a country lane through some vineyards, a little toy I had as a child appeared into my mind for a second or two. I mentioned to my friend what a strange thing it was to me that I would see the little hand-painted, perfume-burning lamp my mother had given to me when I was about eight and lived in Phoenix, Arizona. I proceeded to tell him about some of my other toys, because they had been given to me as antiques. I described one in particular with great detail. It was a blackboard on a folding easel, like an artist would have. The bottom of the blackboard was attached to the easel by hinges, and was secured at the top by a latch which, when released, let the blackboard drop down to become a desktop. At the very top of the easel was a scroll wound by a wooden handle which showed Roman numerals, times tables, geographical names, American presidents, etc. There was something written on that desktop when it was let down. I had been learning hand-writing at school, and I had a favorite word I loved to spell which I wrote with a green crayon across the desktop. 'Mississippi'. My ' ps' were not parallel.

The day progressed, we had a late lunch in Santa Rosa, then took a short stroll. We came upon a large antique co-operative and decided to enter. As I stepped through the threshold, immediately in front of me was a little hand-painted lamp exactly like the one I had been describing. It was setting on a metal painted stove identical to one I'd had. I exclaimed, "That is exactly like my little lamp I was describing! And that is exactly like my little stove, and also that refrigerator there next to it!"

My friend suggested we should look through the rest of the store for any more familiar items. I saw in a display case a bride doll with unmovable arms and legs like one I'd had. I told him, "If I see that blackboard, I will faint." We walked all over looking for it, unsuccessful-ly. Finally leaving, I noticed a storage area with some items in it. We had a discussion and decided to go ahead and take a look. My friend said to me, "If we do see that blackboard, I might be the one to faint." There it was. We were both holding our breaths as I released the latch and let down the desktop. There was my 'Mississippi', with its poorly placed 'ps'.

I don't know how those things got there, and it doesn't matter so much. What I really want to know, is what made me see that little lamp in my mind just a few hours before.

Ashoorian:

For sure it was an ESP experience. Such experiences are considered to be precognition. You suddenly remembered something from decades ago, and a few hours later all that you saw was manifested in front of your eyes. This is the mystery of these kinds of phenomena. One sees or feels events before they happen. The nature of precognition is that it happens spontaneously. I, personally, get an odd feeling, and in my mind I see a short vision or event of which I'm not aware or have not thought about. It crosses my mind for a few seconds and then vanishes. Within a short time the event happens as I felt it.

Priel:

Mr. Ashoorian, would you consider describing some of your ESP occurrences?

Ashoorian:

I've had many such experiences in both awakened state and in dreams. A few have been astounding. I'll share one of them now. For two weeks I had been making daily visits to a dear friend in a hospital near my house. Then, on this particular day, as I was leaving toward the elevator, I got that strange feeling almost like in a trance. I began worriedly looking around in the corridors and stairway, visualizing what could the employees do to help the patients if an earthquake occurred. It all crossed my mind for just several seconds and then vanished. The time from when I got into the elevator and until I arrived home was about seven minutes. As I entered my house, the 1989 Loma Prieta earthquake shook the whole Bay Area. When I visited my friend again, he excitedly exclaimed, "Misha, you can't imagine what it was like here! The nurses were running everywhere pushing us into the corridors, and hurriedly trying to help patients down the stairs! You should have seen it!"

Priel:

That truly is astounding!

Ashoorian:

I'll tell you about a more recent ESP experience which was equally profound and informative. One night I was preparing to go to bed. While I was brushing my teeth, I had one of those feelings I usually get when the information comes through. I heard my own inner voice very vividly whisper, "Something will happen that all the channels will broadcast it." I heard that and in three seconds forgot about it. This is the way that ESP phenomena happen. It gives us a hint and then vanishes. That night was not a good night for me. I was restless and struggling without knowing why. The next morning my son woke me up saying, "Dad, wake up! Come and see what all the channels are showing." I got up and went to the living room. What I saw, was the two World Trade Towers on fire and in smoke. What was shocking to me, was that the words from my inner voice had said almost the same words that my son told me. "Dad... all the channels are showing it ."

Priel:

Amazing! But how could that have been perceived by you? How would you define that? ESP, collective unconscious, or something else?

Ashoorian:

The right definition might be hard to term, but probably it can be classified as premonitions milder than clairvoyance or precognition. The reason for that, is that I did not perceive the towers. I just had this strong feeling that some extraordinary thing is going to happen.

My personal opinion about it is different. The time that I heard my inner voice was almost 11:00 p.m., Pacific Standard time, the night of September 10, 2001. Probably, those people who were going to perform their terrorist action that coming morning were preparing with a great intensity. So, they were putting a great energy in motion, like thought forms, emotions, and so forth, into space. Therefore, I believe that kind of transmission and radiance touches the minds of many sensitive people when their minds are open and channeled to such a phenomenon, and they perceive and get a hint about events. I think that I was one of them.

Priel:

You said previously that you also have ESP in dreams. President Abraham Lincoln had predictive dreams. Some he told to a few of his cabinet members. He had one dream of being in a large hall where he heard a shot and a woman scream. It is stated that on a very particular night he dreamed he saw a man in a coffin. When he asked a soldier guard who it was, he was told that the president had been assassinated. The following night President Lincoln was shot.

I had one recurring dream beginning when I was twelve years old. I would always see the same grand home on an expansive grassy knoll. I would go up and knock at the strong oak door. It would open, and looking across the spacious inside and through French doors, I saw acres of emerald green lawn. In my earlier years I saw that same dream seven or eight times. Forty years later, I owned and lived in that house. Incidentally, that home was built only a few years before I purchased it, and was in a town I had never heard of previously. Yet, that's all there was to it. I simply lived there, and four years later sold it. I cannot understand such a dream happening.

Ashoorian:

Dreams have different aspects. The most important are symbolic and prophetic dreams. I personally have had many symbolic dreams since I was a child. Now I will tell you one of the most astonishing symbolic dreams I have had. It was several decades ago in Iran. On one of those special nights, I dreamed of a great crowd in the yard of our church in Iran. The Assyrian Patriarch was giving a speech on a high balcony. I and my friend, General Phillip Betoshna, of the Shah's army, were standing on the Patriarch's right and left sides. All of a sudden, His Holiness collapsed down off the balcony. I desperately tried to hold him, but I did not succeed. I woke up terrified and perspiring. When morning came, I called General Phillip, and told him about my dream. He was shocked. Hours later in the afternoon, he called and told me with a sad voice that he had just received a telegram from America. His Holiness had been assassinated in San Jose, California. Later, I coordinated the time of the assassination, and it was almost at the same time as when I had the dream in Iran.

Priel:

Certainly, we shouldn't attempt to make something out of every dream that we have, since most are totally meaningless.

Ashoorian:

Basically, dreams which come in the early hours of our sleep are nothing of consequence. Symbolic or prophetic dreams depend on the intensity of the event which is supposed to happen, and have a higher meaning for us. It has been said that most dreams of premonition are about disastrous events, because the intensity causes the dreamer to remember the dramatic effect of it. What I see as important in this type of phenomenon is that we experience something about an event before it happens or as it is being manifested.

Priel:

Regarding all those extrasensory perception occurrences we've been talking about, I feel fairly certain that anyone who has never experienced such a thing must surely not believe they are possible. How is it that some ordinary and logical people spontaneously experience these things, and others do not? Even some people who attempt to do so cannot succeed. Can it be that some are more in balance and in harmony with their feeling about the universe?

Ashoorian:

We are all in harmony with universal law without knowing. I can tell you about something which I think can contribute to being more attuned. The ultimate key is to align ourselves to the principles and cycles of our planet. Here is a picture, in the form of a calculation done by astrologers, which conveys human relationship with the universe. It goes like this.

Some astrologers have made a survey about the human breathing cycle with our planet and solar system. They came up with an average of 16.7 breaths per minute. Now let me tell you what they have done with that. If we multiply 16.7 by 60 minutes to get one hour of breathing, it is equal to 1,002. Then multiply 1,002 by 24 hours of one earth rotation, which is equal to 24,002. That is the average amount of breaths a human takes in 24 hours. As our solar system rotates in the galaxy, it passes through each of the 12 zodiac signs. Taking 2,000 years to pass each one, if we multiply the 2,000 by the 12 signs, it is equal to 24,000 years. That is equal to our 24,000 breaths per our cycle. Just imagine yourself a part of it all, and of being in tune with the universe.

~Meditation~

Priel:

Since most of what is termed extrasensory perception occurs spontaneously, why do some people attempt to derive such experiences by meditating?

Ashoorian:

Extrasensory perception is a phenomenon over which one has no control. It happens spontaneously, but meditation is different. Those who attempt to get some information from the unseen side by meditation have to go through a very different process in order to tap those essential regions which enable them to perceive information or answers to their desired subject.

Priel:

Why is such emphasis placed on silence?

Ashoorian:

There are many old sayings about silence. It has been said, "It is in silence that the soul speaks", or, "in silence you will hear the voice of God", and, "speech is silver, but silence is gold". That is precisely true. Through the silence we link the brain, mind, and soul together. Through the silence we learn to concentrate and relax our body to enable us to meditate and get the deepest level of existence. In silence we learn so much that cannot be described with words, thought, and any other expressions.

Priel:

We act through our conscious mind during our daily life, but we have learned that the human being can function through his superconsciousness in different levels. Does this happen while in a meditative state?

Ashoorian:

Our consciousness is more absolute than anything existing in the physical world. But our superconscious mind is even beyond that, beyond any boundaries that can be imagined. It acts in a very different level faster than the speed of light. It is our higher self. It is you and me, and in the same time it is not. It unites us with divine intelligence of the universe, and enables us to interact in the fourth dimension of extrasensory perception and beyond that. For an ordinary man it would be hard to interact in the superconscious mind, but for a trained meditator it might be accomplished in meditation or in his daily life while he is in a meditative state.

Priel:

How does the process of meditation start? What is the first step one should take?

Ashoorian:

The first phase for meditation is complete relaxation of the body. Without relaxation meditation cannot be accomplished. One has to learn how to relax and sit upright balancing the spine and neck. Another important step is to breathe deeply and silently through the nose. By doing this all the crises, body sensations, thoughts, emotions, and desires will be stilled in a complete silence. This process must be practiced until it can be done unconsciously.

The next phase is concentration. One has to be one pointed and in full control of the mind, still and passive, with no thoughts. Concentration with a one-pointed mind is like a magnifying glass directing sunlight on an object to make it burn. The meditator should strictly concentrate on the subject or object of his meditation.

Priel:

There are different methods of meditation all over the world, from India, Tibet, China, and other Far East countries. How can one choose a suitable method of meditation among all of these?

Ashoorian:

It's true about so many methods, not only from the East and Far East, but the West as well. Just in India there are 112 different methods which have been designed and suggested by Shiva, one of the Trinity Gods of Hinduism. I believe whoever has a desire to meditate can find one method among 112 to suit oneself the best.

Despite of all these different methods, there is one main point which all groups and scholars agree upon and have in common. It is that all the patterns of meditation ultimately will lead them to nirvanic state and the divine realm of universal wisdom.

Priel:

Despite all the books which have been published about meditation, still the majority of Western people don't have a clear understanding about its meaning and purpose.

Ashoorian:

Several decades ago it was so. After 1970, the Indian master, Maharishi Mahesh, came to the United States and introduced Transendental Meditation (TM) to American people. Many were attracted to this new method which was quite suitable for Western countries. There are so many purposes in meditation that they cannot be described in one chapter or two. Just one of the main purposes in meditation is to unite the body, mind and soul to have harmony and become one with the universal law.

Priel:

There are some principles in each method of meditation. Are those principles to be considered as religious principles?

Ashoorian:

As a method, some scholars might have considered them religious principles. But in my opinion, another good purpose of meditation is to expand our knowledge of perception toward the ultimate realities of divine awareness, which has no contradiction with religious principles.

Priel:

I suppose it's difficult to determine when and where human beings began to think about meditation, and how they felt that it was an essential aspect of their life in the first place.

Ashoorian:

Meditation is not something new. It was naturally a real aspect of our life since antiquity. We unconsciously were aware of it, because unconsciously we felt that it is a doorway to our ultimate freedom. Our ancestors found out that in being silent and still, there were moments of bliss that freed them from all kinds of aggression, competition, and tension in their everyday life.

Meditation for me has been always something beyond any kind of an adventure in my life. Since my childhood, I felt something like meditation deep in the core of my being. When I grew up, I realized that is a gift of God.

Priel:

In India there are several phases into which a meditator will pass. Will you explain conventional belief about that?

Ashoorian:

Besides so many different schools and Ashrams, which are places of meditation, there is one method which is more attractive and dramatic for advanced meditators. It progresses in different phases. The lower ones have been considered the material state of mind. They are a preliminary preparation of grounding, relaxation, and breathing. The next stages have been considered formless states of mind, like consciousness of infinite space and of infinite objectless. Then arrives the nirvana state, which is awareness of nothingness. In nirvana it's believed that all our desires and self interest are burned out. Beyond that, there is a rare state called nirodh. It is a state of neither perception, nor nonperception. It is an absolute cessation of consciousness and is extremely difficult to attain. It seems not too many masters have dared to cross its boundaries, because there is the possibility of no return.

Priel:

I understand how meditation can bring a state of relaxation and free the mind, and beyond that it might be used to acquire some kind of knowledge and information from collective unconscious or our higher self. But about the aspect of meditation whereby one seeks nirvana or nirodh, that dramatic elevated state of ecstasy, isn't that time consuming and self indulgent? It seems that having a clean and natural behavior and attitude would adequately align a person for the phenomenon being sought.

Ashoorian:

You've brought up something that is a dangerous aspect of meditation, and about which many famous spiritual teachers have warned aspirants. And that is self delusion. Particularly, in the state of nirodh. It has happened that three famous aspirants reached to that high level of ecstasy. The result was that one of them returned as a vegetable. The second one returned and his life ended in a mental institution, and the third one died in that ecstasy. Anything in the world, when you overdo it, can result in ill effects.

I'll tell you more about the states of meditation. They are:

Concentration

Meditation

Contemplation

Adoration

The first stage, which is concentration, might have been a combination of the four phases of the material state we have briefly described earlier. The second stage is meditation. In meditation one has to concentrate upon one desired object or subject and have a one-pointed mind. For example, let's just suppose the object being chosen is an antique clock. He should start building up in his mind the complete structure of the clock, and keep it for a period of time before his mind's eyes, or in other words, his third eye. He should try to learn as much as he can about every piece of the clock, the type of wood and other materials from which it was made, the mechanism inside of it, and the process of constructing it. If the aspirant keeps his mind continuously one pointed on the object of his meditation, he will gradually learn all the details. It would include the history of the antique clock about which he had no previous knowledge. The nature of meditation is to reveal all the important aspects of the subject in the physical plane. This is considered the mysterious result of meditation — learning without reading any book.

Priel:

That indicates we can learn all we wish about any kind of knowledge and the reality of our life through meditation. If that is the case, it might not be that far from the truth when they say everybody is his own best psychic. What do you think?

Ashoorian:

With a good intention and positive attitude toward meditation we can put the seed of an idea in our mind, ask our highest self, and wait steadily for a while. The answer to our idea will be drawn to our mind by an inner voice, or some other way of perception. That is a reality millions of people have experienced.

Priel:

Contemplation, the third, should be a subtler state of meditation. What will the meditator experience?

Ashoorian:

Contemplation will work with the inner meaning of the subject. If an aspirant could perform the state of meditation and enter the contemplation stage, the subject of the meditation, ie., the clock, will disappear leaving an empty space in the subtler plane. Then contemplation will present the inner meaning and the cause beyond the mystery of the subject. It will form the archetype and pattern from which the clock was made. All this will not come to the aspirant with earthly words. It will be perceived by the aspirant in a subtler form of knowledge.

The last stage is adoration. In adoration the aspirant has reached the ultimate core of his subject or object and become one with it. He will realize that all this type of inspiration has come to him from a very high frequency of divine awareness. Having passed through all these stages, he will lose himself in that perfect knowledge and be united with supreme God. He will realize that those moments are the best moments of his life, and the moments of adoration toward his creator.

Priel:

I have a few more questions about meditation which are different from all the methods you described. The first one is, what is witnessing, or mindfulnes?

Ashoorian:

In witnessing, or mindfulness, a meditator should witness his mind and be a silent observer of its activities and the stream of its thoughts. After a while, the meditator becomes detached from witnessing, and away from all the awareness. This will be the first state that ultimately will lead the meditator to the state of 'no mind'.

Priel:

I encounter quite a few people in a state of having no mind! Seriously, though, how can one reach to the state of 'no mind', without using his mind?

Ashoorian:

There has been some argument among famous teachers about this subject. The argument is that in order to reach the state of 'no mind', one still has to use his mind to get there. The Indian spiritual teacher, Krishnamurti, has put it so beautifully. He says, " Meditation is a state of attention beyond thought." I personally believe that is precisely what meditation should be.

Now that we have reached this far, I'd like to pin point some methods and ideas of masters in different parts of the world. Meditation experiences are all the same, but might be expressed differently in different cultures and traditions. For example, I'll start with the great

Indian master, Osho, whose ideas have been written about in many books on meditation and other philosophies. He believes that when you are not doing anything bodily or mentally, and when all activity has ceased, you are simply just…'being'. That, is what meditation is.

In Hinduism, devotion to a divine being is the most popular form of worship and meditation. For Japanese Buddhists, repeating special chanting which leads them to their ultimate state of the mind is their ideal. Hassidic Jews, through dancing and singing, are taken to their highest level of ecstasy. A Buddhist monk, by staring at a blank wall, or by concentrating his mind on a void, or emptiness, takes himself to a nirvanic state.

Another Eastern philosophy about meditation is to mentally die in the past, and be reborn in the present and now. Because past is history, and future is scary and unpredictable. The only real moment in life is this very present moment.

There are other methods. Transcendental Meditation uses the method of a mantra to be repeatedly chanted in order to bring the mind to one pointedness and transcendent for a perfect state of meditation. In the mindfulness method, the mind is witnessing its own activities and the stream of its thoughts. After a while, the meditator becomes detached from witnessing, away from all the awareness, and soars in the nirvanic state.

In Tibetan Buddhism, if one develops the insight method of meditation to emptiness, he will reach a final stage of nirvanic state called Buddhisattva, which means 'awakened state'. This will lead him to return to the world and help humanity towards salvation.

George I. Gurdjieff, another teacher, from Russia, brought his esoteric method school to the West in the first part of the twentieth century. He believed that the human being is asleep and lives a life of automatic, suffering due to attachment to earthly pleasures and unwanted desires, like the Buddhism belief. One should learn the act of observing oneself not in solitary, but among people and nature in order to transpire and liberate himself from the bondage of the world.

Krishnamurti was the genius spiritual teacher of India. He was educated in England under the guidance of Annie Besant, of the Theosophist spiritual sect, in the first part of the twentieth century. He opposed almost all kinds of techniques. He believed using no technique can free the mind. His system, was no system. Each individual should find his own system which suits him best. For him, meditation is a state of attention beyond thoughts, and should be always practiced in the present moment with mindfulness and self knowledge.

Priel:

What is the significance of voicing the sound of A-U-M, which some people do when they meditate?

Ashoorian:

One of the most dramatic styles of meditation is repeating the sound of AUM. Some think that the sound of AUM is the sound of the universe in motion. It has been said that if one goes out of town in the middle of the night and sits in silence on the top of a high hill, listening to the sound of the sphere, he will hear the sound of AUM, believed to be the sound of stars and planets in motion. Some like to meditate to the sound of a distant river flowing over huge rocks, sounding like AUM.

Often a group of monks will sit together chanting the sound of AUM. They repeat it in such a way, each taking breaths at their individual necessity, causing no break in the continuity of sound. They continue until they are absorbed into the sound, and enter into an ecstatic level of the nirvanic state.

In Hinduism the sound of AUM has been considered as cosmic vibration which has three different aspects: A the beginning, U the middle, and M the end. It is chanted in three syllables, A-U-M .

Priel:

The method probably most people equate with meditation is Yoga. It's quite popular in America, and involves the use of various physical positions in order to bring about specific benefits. What is its history?

Ashoorian:

Yoga is more than 5,000 years old and has had many different branches, some of which are no longer practiced. More than a half dozen of them are still very popular, and have been practiced all around India and other countries. It is believed that the root of yoga has come from shamanism. It seems that shamans have had some kinds of rituals practiced to energize their body in order to perform their divinations. It is believed that during the ages those became the basic patterns for today's yoga.

Priel:

What, actually, does the word 'yoga' mean?

Ashoorian:

The word 'yoga' means, in short, 'union', and its method and postures are to transcend our minds to a state of union with universal law. It will harmonize and balance our physical and spiritual aspects of our daily life with all existence.

Priel:

Can you give us the names and explain some of the main postures?

Ashoorian:

Yoga's benefits are so important, and there is so much to be told. In this writing I can give very brief explanations of the main postures. Each specific body positioning has a special purpose.

Hatha yoga, brings our body to a state of health and a balance of our energy through the seven chakras of our body.

Raja yoga, transcends the mind and controls our breath in meditation to attain a higher state.

Karma yoga, is the path which teaches us to move out of egoism, and gives us guidance towards spiritual principles.

Jnana yoga, is the path towards the wisdom to learn to distinguish the real from unreal.

Tantra yoga, is the path of self transcendence to understand that there is no gap between the divine awareness and our physical world. Tantra yoga has been misunderstood by some who have the impression that it consists exclusively of sexual positions, which is not true.

I have to add that in general, yoga is a universal art. Not a kind of religion as has been considered by a minority. Moreover, a most significant part of yoga is breathing and breath control for balancing our energy. As the great theosophist, Helena Blavatsky, put it, the knowledge of the rise and fall of the breath is the highest of those sciences. I believe it happens when, in yoga meditation, one eliminates the concept of time and concentrates on the posture of his body. At that state, time will cease to exist. That is the eternal 'now', the state of samadhi or nirvana, in which the yogis become one with super divine awareness.

Priel:

It might take years for someone to analyze and learn the different methods of meditation.

Ashoorian:

To acquire the perfect art of meditation might require a lifetime. But, in fact, the intention of all the masters and schools of meditation is to transform and guide humanity toward a spiritual path for their salvation. Therefore, a minor difference between some of them is of very little importance. Again, it should be whatever is successful for each individual. Meditation is the greatest adventure in human life. In my opinion, every single individual should experience it, because ultimately it will lead us to the divine wisdom of the universal intelligence and self realization.

Priel:

Do you think it happened that many of the prophets, saints, and great masters of the world used meditation as a path?

Ashoorian:

I really feel that. If you will remember, that is exactly what happened in Buddha's life. To those who have transformed themselves toward enlightenment and a spiritual path, love and compassion will become their permanent nature. They will defuse themselves from all the bad habits of their life, and infuse into themselves an awakened state of mind toward a new, ultra subtle dimension of life the way Buddha did.

Priel:

Earlier, you talked about Chakra, and the seven vital energy centers. According to those teachings, there is a place between our eyebrows called the third eye, which is a dramatic center for concentration. Where are the other chakras located?

Ashoorian:

Chakras are an ancient model for awakening and balancing our energy through meditation, which works like a vortex through seven centers of our body. Focusing on a particular one can help to bring about a certain desired result. I'll briefly give definitions of their characteristics and explain their locations.

The first chakra is located at the base of the spine. It has the quality of solidity and physical survival. It is unconsciously developed most intensely from ages one to seven. We all know how a child through that time frame is mostly concentrating not only on learning the stability of its own body, but in recognizing its place in the environment as well.

The second chakra, called the sex chakra, is located a little higher than the base chakra, and in the front of the body. At this center, sexual desire is prominent, and our first feelings of pleasurable thoughts for the opposite sex begin to ripen there at ages seven to fourteen. Who doesn't recall the wonderment of those feelings, and the curiosity?

The third chakra is located at the naval area, and called the solar plexus. This center has to do with emotion, principles, and discipline. From age fourteen to twenty one there is a struggle to acquire these qualities, and one begins to understand values and how choices should be made.

The fourth chakra is located at the breast bone. We experience the quality of gentleness and sympathy at this center, because it is the path of the heart, full of real love and compassion. It is most profoundly developed from the ages of twenty one to twenty eight, and when a person loves at this age it is a very intense love.

Fifth chakra is located at the throat area. At this center we experience the art of self expression. The greatest aspect of it is the spoken word. As it has been said, when God spoke the word, the universe was created. The four lower chakras, which are more physical, have their activity expressed by the throat center. This becomes more developed from twenty eight to thirty five. For myself, personally, my experience at that age in the artistic time of my life of writing, acting, and speaking, was my most golden period. Many of the greatest writers and composers were the most dynamic at that age.

The sixth chakra is located between the eyebrows, and is one of the most important chakras. It is called our third eye, the eye of the soul.

We are developing ourselves to experience the hidden reality beyond the physical world through visualization by our third eye. When we close our eyes and concentrate at our third eye, the entire power of our physical eyes is converted and transferred to the third eye area. By this, we can see images, patterns, and places that we have never seen or experienced before in our life. This is a creative center where we can contemplate and solve our concerns.

Seventh chakra is located at the crown of the head. It is the highest frequency center through which we are inspired by pure, divine energy to express ourselves in different aspects of our life. By developing this center, we are almost completing the process of our personal evolution, because we are using the experiences of all the other six centers to accomplish the union of being one with our creator.

Priel:

When a person concentrates on a specific chakra during meditation, might he also have a purpose to heal himself of some kind of physical condition related to that center, as well as to deriving the energy from it?

Ashoorian:

Yes. For instance, through the third chakra a pregnant mother, who is connected through her navel to her baby, receives solar energy through that solar plexus on to her child. We have to keep in mind that not all difficult situations or illnesses we experience in our life are caused by other people or external events. Particularly, our malady might be due to an imbalance of our chakras. So, when we concentrate on the concerning imbalance, we are transmuting the energies from the lower level of our body to the highest level and healing the illness of imbalance. When this has been accomplished, one has achieved the union which yogis talk about.

Priel:

There so many philosophies and practices to make life better. What is the simplest and best as far as you are concerned?

Ashoorian:

There is one old Chinese saying:

> To be hard like a diamond,
> Flexible like a willow tree,
> Soft like water,
> And open like space.

I personally believe that if one interacts according to those principles, he will never be a failure in his life.

Phenomena

of

Wonder

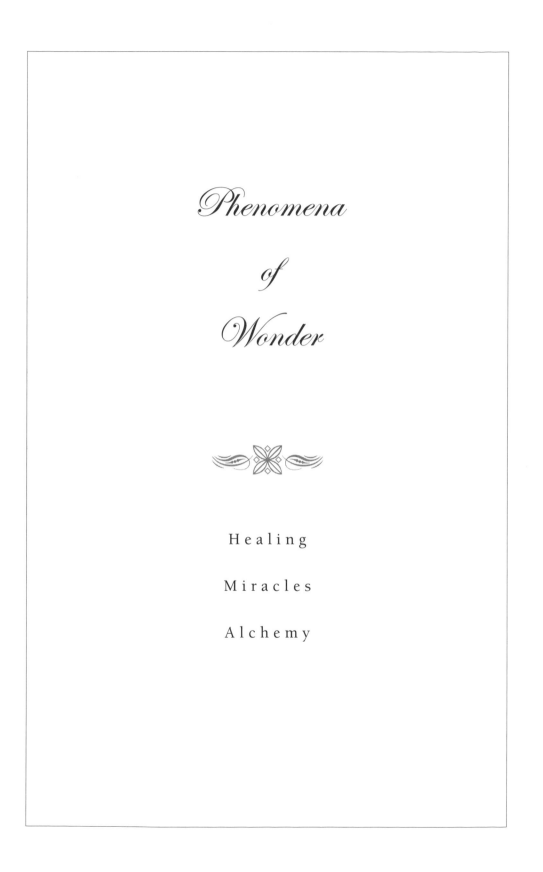

Healing

Miracles

Alchemy

~H e a l i n g~

Priel:

Healing is an enormous subject in metaphysical studies. It is generally thought that healing is done naturally through the energies surrounding the body. You mentioned some of that when you discussed auras. It is also thought that healing is accomplished through belief in divine communication. As far back as history goes, there are references to healing. You must know a great deal about it. What can you tell us about healing through the ages?

Ashoorian:

When we trace the history of healers such as shamans, wise men, high priests, and other healers from early times, we see that a divine art of healing, or gift of God, existed. There is no doubt about that. Even in modern times there are major healing practices all over. They include churches, nature camps, and other concentration groups, some of which have healers who are highly active and famous in the world.

Priel:

What kind of healers are they, I mean, what means are they claiming to use for curing their patients?

Ashoorian:

There are quite a few different methods and practices. Some have techniques of laying on of hands. Some are spiritual healers. Some use herbals as their technique. Crystal amplifies energy, and is used by some to increase the vibrations of their energy towards their patient. Others use psychological therapy, and so forth. Of course, we cannot forget that in both early and modern times there have been deceptive people claiming the ability to heal.

Priel:

Saints are exceptional people who have been proclaimed to be in an exalted position by some of the Christian churches. What about healing by saints, and prophets of antiquity?

Ashoorian:

Prophets like Moses, Buddha, or Mohammed, as far as I know, have not had any major healing activities written about in scriptures. The only prophet who has many major healings recorded is Jesus of Nazareth in the New Testament, and after him, his disciples. Of course, parallel to that era there were spiritual healers in India, Assyria, Persia, Egypt, Palestine, and other countries who did miraculous healing. Probably we might talk about some of them later on.

Priel:

As you mentioned earlier, the word 'miracle', is a Latin derivative meaning, 'to wonder at'. Tell us about the method for healings performed by Jesus.

Ashoorian:

In my opinion, Jesus' soul was not an ordinary soul, therefore his ability for healing should not be an ordinary means like ordinary healers. He was aware and born with healing power. He had power over four elements of nature, i.e., fire, air, water, and earth. In the New Testament we can see how he demonstrated his power over four elements plus spirit.

Priel:

Can you be more specific about using and having power over four elements and spirit?

Ashoorian:

Let me allegorically describe it according to New Testament writing. For instance, when Jesus took some soil from the ground and mixed it with water and rubbed it on the eyes of a blind man, he used earth element to heal him. At the time of fishing with his disciples when he calmed the stormy waves of the Sea of Galilee, he used the water element. At the last moment of his crucifixion he caused the stormy weather as a heavenly sign, using the air element. The fourth one is fire. Fire is living energy equal to soul. For raising a man by the name of Lazarus from the dead, he used fire element. Last but not least, on the final day, he initiated his disciples with the Holy Spirit and gave them the power, saying, "Whatever you tied on Earth will be tied in Heaven, and whatever is untied by you on Earth will be untied in Heaven as well." This is the realm of spirit. Jesus was the essence of divine awareness.

Priel:

In the cases of Jesus' healing process, was the faith of the patient supposed to be essential?

Ashoorian:

In the case of an ordinary healer, the faith of the patient might be a lot of help and might accelerate and open the channel between the two of them. But in Jesus' case, I think it was not essential. We read in scriptures that most of the patients were not even present, and some like the blind man did not want to go to Jesus to be healed. In spite of all that, when the healed persons were thanking Jesus, he would tell them to rise, that their faith had healed them. So faith is a great factor for the patient to be healed.

Priel:

Among tribal healers, the job of healing was passed down in their families for generations of healing. Was it thought a healing ability is genetically inherited in a family?

Ashoorian:

Not necessarily a family's genetic inheritance, but a gift of God of the healer's personality and the genetic make up which draws him toward devoting his life for healing the sick people. I see what you are thinking, though, since creative talents and other characteristics are inherent from generation to generation. You cause me to think about my own daughter and how she has predictive dreams like I do. Sometimes it is uncanny how we both will be thinking the same thing.

Priel:

What else would a spiritual healer need to have in order to be successful?

Ashoorian:

Faith and an active imagination to direct oneself beyond the physical, where the realm of divine awareness is making everything possible.

Priel:

Skeptics argue that the power of mind or of spirit cannot possibly heal and dissolve a physical tumor which clinically cannot be cured.

Ashoorian:

All existing matter is the product of spirit. This is not to mean spirit as beings, but as all energies and divine essence. It is beyond words to describe how a spiritual healer is projecting his subjective energy onto the substances of the physical illness and directing the illness toward the healing process. All these are happening and are governed beyond the physical realm.

Priel:

Would mental illness be easier to cure from a distance than physical illness would be?

Ashoorian:

It depends on the degree of the illness and the rank of the spiritual healer. A healer of high rank can heal the patient from a distance even if the patient is unaware and has no faith. Dervishes heal their patients by the power of words and their Zikr. They believe that their breath or voice travels through the ether level to any distance and heals the patient. The mastery of dervishes is to project their power of mind like an electric current to anywhere they desire, no matter how far the distance.

Priel:

There is a belief that the cause of all illnesses, mental and physical, results from imbalances in our body's energy and aura. If that is true, how can one who is suffering cure himself?

Ashoorian:

All types of illnesses are the result of imbalance in our body's energy. Sometimes we are creating a sort of negative thought forms in our astral level which eventually will cause different illnesses either mentally or physically. Those who want to cure themselves should, in the name of God and universal intelligence, create a great desire and get above their illness to cure themselves.

Priel:

The method of healing through prayer has been the most popular in the world, despite all other methods today. Why is that?

Ashoorian:

Healing by prayer and faith has been proven to have more effect on the patient than a physical healer who directs his own power without relying on a divine aspect of the universe. It has been noticed that mothers praying with great desire for healing their children have had more effect than any medicine. In prayer, one has to be connected by great love and sympathy with that source of his being which is connected to the spark of divine realm.

Priel:

Are all spiritual healers believing that the healing process is happening out of time and space?

Ashoorian:

All the real spiritual healers admit that to cure an illness requires an intelligence superior to humans', that of total knowledge of the physical law.

Priel:

Are they saying that is the power of God?

Ashoorian:

Term it whatever you wish. The spiritual healer is convinced that at the time of healing he is surrounded by angelic forces and he is just as an instrument through which to cure his patient.

Priel:

Some believe that healing is natural. Others believe that it is super-natural.

Ashoorian:

It is an art and a science. It is a miraculous phenomenon because it is happening in a supernormal realm beyond our known physical laws. All the miracles and healings are in God's realm and are happening directly from God or from an angelic dimension. Sometimes it might happen that a patient is not healed due to not being in an appropriate condition, or for a karmic reason from his or her past life.

Priel:

What about self healing? What about a person who sits quietly, trying to feel all the universe around him, trying to feel the goodness move through his body to take away the illness? Would that simple plea be responded to? Would the elements around him penetrate through the body to heal it?

Ashoorian:

In the most simple way, that is what is happening. Provided, that there is faith, faith, and only faith. When we are in gross body and conscious of everything around us we are continuously evaluating our thoughts and reacting accordingly. This is the physical realm in which the self healing process is almost impossible. But as we said earlier, if we step out of our self into a different realm, we will be in a transcendental dimension, in a different ecstatic realm. That is the faith domain in which those essential elements will penetrate our body and accomplish the process of self healing.

Priel:

Who are considered to have been the most famous healers?

Ashoorian:

Mystic healers of ancient times and of the Renaissance era have had miracles and endless healings written about them. In the twentieth century, one of the most famous psychic healers was Edgar Cayce. We have stated before that he was an American, who was called "the sleeping prophet". He received information through hypnotic trances which diagnosed and recommended treatments for illnesses. Thousands of people were healed by following the mostly herbal treatments recommended. Scientists performed many experiments on him to determine how he could have such a success rate. They found nothing which could disprove what he claimed. He was instrumental through his herbal remedies in bringing about alternative medicine.

At the time, Edgar Cayce was internationally the center of attention among hundreds of other psychic healers and the New Age movement. His ability in healing was performed from collective universal intelligence. He described each individual as a trinity of body, mind, and spirit. His method was like the ancients, because he was able to scan the body of his patients and diagnose their illness from a distance. Beyond the healing information he received through trances, he received information about many subjects from the distant past and into the future.

Another healer, Harry Edwards, the famous spiritual healer in Great Britain, is called one of the greatest healers of the world. He has healed hundreds of people in hospitals and other institutions all over England. His belief is that the actual cause for most types of cancers is not physical. His claim is that mostly it is not viral and not a question of infection at all, and that it is purely a matter of psychological frustration.

Thomas Johnson, another prominent psychic medium and healer of Great Britain, is the director of a spiritualist association in

England. He believes that during the time of healing some spiritual forces around him are helping and assisting him in the healing process.

Barbara Ann Brennan is another gifted healer of America with many decades of experience. She has observed more than 5,000 clients. Her belief is that our bodies exist within a larger 'body', a human energy field, or aura, through which we have access to that power to heal ourselves and others.

Probably the most famous worldwide is Sai Baba, the avatar of India. He is claimed to be the third reincarnation of Sai Baba. It was predicted in Hindu scriptures thousands of years ago that he would be the one who becomes the great avatar of the twentieth century. Many professors from different countries have devoted years of their life to promoting Sai Baba's teachings. They believe that he is a real avatar and has a special Christ soul. Some believe that he has healed thousands of people from all around the world who went to his ashram. They received special healing ashes produced in the palms of his hand from out of the air. It is said that he has millions of followers all around the world.

The main aspect of his healing is his spiritual doctrine that love is the way to true wisdom, and that unconditional love and compassion transcend wisdom. There are many informative books written by his followers about his life and the healing and miracles he performed.

Priel:

What about the eras of the Dark Ages and the Renaissance? For instance, it is recorded that the Rosicrucian masters also were healers. What about them?

Ashoorian:

The Rosicrucians were great alchemists, and have done miraculous healing during the last three centuries. Their high-ranking masters were very educated physicians and alchemists who had access to a kind of medicine which they called universal medicine. It is recorded that their physicians cured emperors and queens from incurable diseases by that universal medicine which they produced with the art of alchemy.

Priel:

You have given amazing material to us. We all wish for the possibility that every human on the earth might be able to find comfort, health, and peace from simple surrender to the goodness of the universe.

~Miracles~

Priel:

Reports about miraculous healing and other events are puzzling to people in our modern societies. Some have come up with the idea that the process is from virtual level to physical, in other words, like quantum physics.

Ashoorian:

Miracles are not happening only from the virtual level through quantum to physical level. Sometimes they are happening backward from the physical level through quantum to virtual level. The story of that man who was traveling with his twelve year old daughter in Arizona will be a good example.

They were driving for hours on a long highway when their small truck had a technical problem. He pulled out onto the shoulder, lifted the truck with a small jack he had, and lay down under the truck. Unfortunately, this jack could not hold in the sandy shoulder of the road, and the truck collapsed on his body. He began screaming and crying for help. His daughter was shocked and frozen, not knowing what to do! Deadly moments were passing by, while the man was continuously screaming for help. Suddenly the girl, while she was in an abnormal condition, approached the truck, put her hand under the bumper, and lifted the truck from her father's body, saving him from that deadly situation. Later on, the man told his story to many people and the newspapers. Some believed. Some did not, and asked how could that happen for a twelve year old girl to lift a truck, even a small truck, off her father…it's impossible!

Priel:

I ask the same question. I've read of other feats happening when the person is experiencing tremendous shock and stress. How really could that happen? That's impossible from a physical point of view.

Ashoorian:

You are right. In the physical level it is impossible. But what made the twelve year old girl lift that small truck was a miracle that happened in a different dimension. Miracles are not happening the way that most people think. The patterns of miracles are already there in an invisible dimension. One has to step out of the collective human condition and be in accordance with the right universal law. Then the miracles will happen. That was unconsciously happening to that girl. Her great desire to help her father, and the pleas of her father to be saved, transported both of them to an intense ecstatic level beyond the physical realm. In such a high frequency level the subject of weight loses its concept, unknown energies are brought forth which alter the gravity, the boundaries of separation disappear, and everything becomes one. At those heavenly moments the power of the universe moved through both of them and made the impossible, possible. That is backward quantum physics, from physical level to virtual level. Moreover, with faith, good intention, and being with God, everything is possible. As I said earlier, God acts mysteriously and never leaves footsteps of its action.

Priel:

Some people fervently and absolutely believe in miracles, and others absolutely scoff at the mere suggestion of anything being miraculous.

Ashoorian:

I've mentioned well-known situations. But now I want to tell you about some healing and miraculous activities which I personally witnessed or have heard about from a trusted priest and others who have been present at the times of their happening. It has convinced me beyond any doubt that miracles can happen in abnormal conditions. There was a great holy man by the name of Mar Yosip, from our Assyrian Church of the East. He was really considered a holy man by both Christians and Moslems of his area. He was born in 1893, in the northern part of Iraq in a small village called Harir, where he lived until the day he passed away in 1977, at the age of 84. The patriarchal position began in his family from the sixteenth century A.D., and ended in 1975. He was to have been patriarch, but passed the position to his nephew, Holiness Mar Eshai Shemon, the last patriarch of the same dynasty, who was assassinated in San Jose. Mar Yosip performed most of his healing and miracles in his mountain village. The healing and miracles performed by him are unbelievable, especially by modern man in such a high tech century of today.

Priel:

If you have been a witness yourself, and have heard from reliable priests, you simply must tell us more about it.

Ashoorian:

This holy man was an extraordinarily simple person, and some believed that he was not aware of his power that he possessed. I will describe some of what I have seen and heard. He would go to the houses of sick poor people of his area, and lay his hand on the patient and pray in his Assyrian Aramaic language. The patient would be healed instantly, or by the morning for sure. My mother-in-law suffered from severe migraines. Whenever she got it, it took three days to get rid of the killing pain.

One evening I was invited to her house with many other family members. She approached Mar Yosip and kneeled in front of him, describing her terrible migraine. In his usual manner, he lay his hand over her head and prayed with a loud voice. My mother-in-law never once had that headache again, living for another forty years. Thousands of healings of this type and even more serious illnesses were attributed to him. Other miracles he performed are unbelievable. Yet, believe it or not, they are true.

One year in the countryside, all the farms were attacked by locusts which were covering and eating all the crops. The government and farmers could do nothing to drive them away. Farmers knew that Mar Yosip was their only resort, to work his miracles and solve the problem. They went to the Ministry of Agriculture and told their situation. They talked about many other miracles that Mar Yosip had performed. The minister officially asked Mar Yosip to help the farmers. It has been claimed by hundreds of people who were witnesses that day, that Mar Yosip stood on top of a hill, raised his hands praying, and with a loud voice said, "You insects, the creatures of God, leave this place and never come back again." After a few seconds, in front of the stunned minister and hundreds of other witnesses, the locusts rose into the sky like a black cloud and flew toward the mountain and disappeared. That event was broadcasted many times on the radio programs the same day, and people of Iraq and Syria still talk about it even now.

Some more miracles were performed by Mar Yosip which many priests have witnessed. They say that sometimes they traveled with him from one village to another. In the deep valleys of the mountains wild animals like wolves and coyotes would follow and try to attack. Mar Yosip would stay behind and stretch his hands toward the wild animals, chanting some words. After a while, the wild animals would approach and sit in front of him, and quietly put their heads on the ground between their two front feet. He would turn and join the men, saying, "Well, boys, let's go. They are resting for a while." The priests say they would walk away and look back at the wild animals still resting until they disappeared from sight.

Priel:

One would not think the priests would have anything to gain from telling such stories.

Ashoorian:

According to many priests, some of whom are in the United States, and one being the priest of my church in San Jose, California, they have witnessed such astonishing things performed by him that I do not even dare to talk about them here.

He was not using any technique to accomplish anything. He was not even aware of that divine power which he possessed. He thought it was happening naturally because he was simply praying and asking with love and great compassion to help others. His pure intention and faith in God and Jesus Christ made everything possible for him.

Priel:

What you've described leads me to relate something I recently heard which was also witnessed, and recorded and authenticated. It goes like this. Born in 1603, in Copertino, Italy, Joseph Desa was a Franciscan Catholic friar. While praying or in a state of rapturous spiritual thought, oblivious to all which was around him, he often would be raised into the air. It happened scores of times. This levitation occurred in churches large and small, in the open air, in front of large gatherings, and was seen by Pope Urban VIII. He sometimes caught up someone in his arms to float around the room with him, including some who became healed. Lambs surrounded him when he prayed, and sparrows responded to his commands. Such large crowds gathered to see him that he was sent to live in seclusion in the remote countryside. It is considered that his "supernatural happenings" are on a scale unparalleled by any other authenticated saints.

Ashoorian:

To close this subject, here are a few more words. Miracles are a phenomenon happening by the help of some invisible power in nature which, some believe, is conducted by some being in an angelic dimension and with the power of faith of the person who is involved. All these powers are rooted in human psyche. Jesus said, "Ask, and it will be given."

Priel:

I want to say something that is about a kind of miracle, and is analogous of a real miracle. It is the miracle of a book. It is so small you can hold it in your hands, and it weighs hardly anything. A caveman could have seen it and never have fathomed that upon opening it we are provided with knowledge of the world and the universe. Man has made a kind of miracle! You said that God is only one step outside ourselves. That should mean that knowledge of all there is, is only one step away; and, therefore, we can simply, like opening a book, open that door to step through to embrace all the secrets of the universe.

~A l c h e m y~

Priel:

Alchemy is a subject about which I have read very little, because I had an impression that alchemy was almost another word for the kind of magic associated with wizards in fiction. I understand that it has to do with chemical formulas. I have so much respect for your studies and research, that I see there must be much more to be said about it if you have taken the time and made the effort to read about it. Is there any tangible evidence existing regarding alchemy's status?

Ashoorian:

There remain today hundreds of alchemical formulas written by alchemists and wise men of ancient and medieval times. Alchemy at its highest was for the purpose of discovering the 'matter' of life—the original substance in the universe and man. Through several thousand years it took a number of directions and showed up in other practices and philosophies. Sometimes stories and legends arose, and sometimes pretenders. The most tangible evidence of alchemy is by a famous alchemist by the name of Wenzel Seiler. He had the most evident performance of manufacturing gold from base metal while in the presence of the emperor of Germany and Hungary. Seiler took a large object of silver and dipped the bottom part into his elixir. It transmuted the bottom part of the metal into the purist of gold, and the top of it remained silver. This object is preserved in Vienna, in the imperial treasury chamber. It is stated that this metal, consisting originally of silver, has been partly transmuted into gold by alchemical means. Afterward, Wenzel Seiler was knighted by King Leopold I, and given the title, Wenzeslous Ritter Von Reinburg, In the Promoas of the Temple of Wisdom.

Priel:

You mentioned that Rosicrucians had a universal medicine which was produced by alchemy. It is noted that since times of old there have been wise men who made an elixir for healing, and which they used for manufacturing gold from base metal. Others in the course of history have confirmed the actuality of this. The processing of copper and tin to make bronze, and iron and carbon to make steel, might have made the processing of gold appear a possibility. Such a thing would be difficult to believe for people of today. Could you describe it in some simple words?

Ashoorian:

It's a complicated process, but I will try my best. Alchemy was a mysterious science of multiplication. The main philosophy of it is based upon natural growth. The ancient masters believed that the essence of God (the universe) is within everything, and through it growth manifests itself in all else. That is the natural law in the universe, increasing and improving. They believed that the greatest miracle is in the seed of a mustard. When it is planted it grows and produces thousands of times larger than the size of the seed itself. That is the undeniable process of growth in nature. So, the rationale is if this is possible for a seed of mustard, why shouldn't the seed of gold in base metal be multiplied thousands of times to grow pure gold by the art of alchemy. This is not my saying. That is what all the alchemists of olden times believed and were said to have actually performed.

Priel:

What do they mean by the seed of gold? Where did the seed of gold come from, and where was it to be planted in order to grow?

Ashoorian:

Within everything, is the seed of everything else. It has been said that every grain of sand contains the seed of all that exists in the universe. In alchemical terminology, the seed of gold was any base metal. It was nourished in a special material by a mysterious alchemical process.

Priel:

Who were those people working in that manner? Base metal turning into gold is a process that takes nature millions of years.

Ashoorian:

Alchemy was a chemical way of accelerating the process. I need to talk about those alchemy masters in order to make it clear for some people who have the impression that alchemists were performing a type of magic. Rosicrucian masters and all other alchemists were very educated people who had tremendous knowledge about chemicals and all other elements in nature. Besides that, they were strongly spiritual and possessed the wisdom of the universe.

Alchemy is thought to have originated in Egypt. Some think it developed also in Mesopotamia, Phoenicia, India, China, Persia and other nations practicing and performing this art. After Arabs conquered Egypt in the seventh century A.D., their scholars adapted it and put in process their own alchemical medicine. Later on, from Arabia this art was transported to Europe and other neighboring countries.

Priel:

What was the basic material an alchemist would begin with?

Ashoorian:

The alchemist was using primal elements, called the 'first matter', which after a special process was converted to a pliable form called philosopher's stone. Although, it was not a stone at all. Philosophers and scientists were considered almost the same thing at that time, because philosophers were involved with trying to determine and understand the nature of life. The stone's real quality was not revealed, except to highly ranked alchemists. There are some who speculate this prime material might be that from which all life has come into existence.

Making the first matter began with lengthy and complicated processing and combining the prime material of sea salt and certain forms of sulfur and mercury essences. The clearest sea salt would be taken from the sea and dried up in a stove, then ground to a very fine powder. During the months of May and June when the moon is full, they would place specially designed glass receptacles in some particular areas, possibly where the air was best, or in the areas of certain mineral springs. In the daytime, sulfur of the solar rays, which they called divine fire, descended. At night, the emanations of it rises, and the mercury of the lunar rays came in contact to combine and condense. That became a partly tangible substance forming the purest of dew, uncontaminated, and making the essential virgin ground in which to begin the work.

Priel:

Then what did they do?

Ashoorian:

The dew the alchemist collected in the glass containers was placed in the sun for many weeks until it showed a kind of roots like germination at the bottom of the bottle. When manipulated by distillation in an alchemist lab, it produced a mysterious oil which was a secret known only by alchemists and wise men. Next, the sea salt was mixed with that material. That all had to be heated in special lab tubes under a controlled heat for a long time. There were fourteen procedures to be accomplished until an elixir was produced. To perform such a difficult work, alchemists had to patiently proceed and be careful with the heating of the material. Without the right knowledge and expertise, the danger of a great explosion in the lab from overheating could cause a devastating situation and take his life. It is a reality which has happened more than once in the course of the history. It might require years to reach the perfect state to produce the legendary elixir capable not only to transmute base metal to gold, but to cure all kinds of illnesses. Some thought it could give eternal youth.

Priel:

I can understand how some of the ingredients could be flammable or explosive when heated.

Ashoorian:

Much more than that, if that material in the lab tube was developed too far from what it is supposed to be heated, it could seep and disappear, there being no physical container existing in the world to be strong enough to hold it; because that material was no longer a substance, but a divine essence unknown to ordinary man.

Priel:

I don't like to sound like a skeptic, but most believe that alchemy is speculation of abnormal people who deluded themselves and never could produce such an elixir in their life. What do you say about that?

Ashoorian:

I would say that alchemy is much more than speculation. It existed at the time of Hermetists. The science of Hermes was a reality like all other science. Those who were witnesses at the time of transmutation of base metal into gold have declared that the gold which was produced was more pure and precious than gold in the mines of the earth.

Priel:

Who are other people considered as famous alchemists of the ancient and modern worlds?

Ashoorian:

There have been many. In ancient times, a very notable one was Pythagoras of Greece. Famous in more recent centuries is Sir Isaac Newton, whose hand-written formula about alchemy is still kept in one of Europe's great libraries. Thomas Norton, Basil Valentine, and St. Germain are some more. The most legendary alchemist of all is Paracelsus, who had great knowledge about nature's spirits and other inhabitants of the invisible world. It is said that he learned the secret knowledge of Brahmans in India. He cured people, healed leprosy, cancer, and other illnesses. He performed many miracles, and at the end of his life by the art of alchemy made a lot of gold. Some of his friends and followers believed that he lived for two hundred years and stayed young as the result of his knowledge of the holy science of alchemy.

Priel:

You said alchemists were spiritual. Some think alchemy was a spiritual process. What about that?

Ashoorian:

All the real alchemists and wise men were spiritual people. Those legendary people with such mastery and spirit would have had access to all the knowledge of the world, and no doubt they transformed their base human nature to a very high level of spirituality. Despite all the different ideas and beliefs, there is one definite reality that in the course of all that history there have been many kings, high priests, and other scientists who witnessed the miraculous process of metallic transformation.

Believe it or not, King Henry IV, of England, prohibited the production of gold and silver by the use of alchemy, because he was afraid that the gold value of the country would have been devalued.

Priel:

I've heard it was said that some deceased masters would appear to an alchemy disciple and reveal to him the secret of the last necessary substance for processing the alchemical art. Was that intended to be allegorical?

Ashoorian:

It was not allegorical. Some alchemists would purposely eliminate one final substance from their formula to be sure that their disciple could find it by himself. That would prove he was qualified to be initiated as an alchemist. It was told that after some other masters passed away they would appear to their disciples and reveal the final substance of the last stage of processing, or warn them of its potential danger. I'll quote from Paul Roland's book, *Revelations Wisdom of the Ages,* about an event which was to have happened in the twentieth century:

"Although it is believed that Fulcanelli died in 1932, several men claimed to have met him in mysterious circumstances over the next twenty years and each time the alchemist appeared younger than before! In 1937, seven years before the development of the atomic bomb, Jacques Bergier, research assistant to the French atomic physicist Andre Helbronner, was approached by a man he believed to be Fulcanelli in a Paris laboratory warning of the dangers of the "… liberation of atomic energy", which alchemists claimed to have known about for a very long time."

There is a real mystery to alchemy. Unfortunately, alchemy was almost dead by the beginning of the twentieth century. After years of my curiosity about the holy aspect in the art of alchemy, I read one thing that has amazed and fascinated me the most, and I want to quote it from Manly P. Hall's book entitled, *The Secret Teachings of All the Ages*. He states:

"If two persons, one an initiate and the other nunilluminated in the supreme art, were to set to work side by side, using the same vessels, the same substances, and exactly the same modus operandi, the initiate would produce his "gold" and the uninitiated would not. Unless the greater alchemy has first taken place within the soul of man, he cannot perform the lesser alchemy in the retort. This is an invariable rule, although it is cunningly hidden in the allegories and emblems of Hermetic philosophy. Unless a man be "born again" he cannot accomplish the Great Work, and if the student of alchemical formulae will remember this, it will save him much sorrow and disappointment."

It is a pure reality that from two alchemists, one initiated and spiritual could produce the elixir of eternal medicine while the other one could not. It is unfortunate that the concept of spirituality has not yet been comprehended by the majority of people even in the twenty first century. Mr. Hall has dramatically penetrated the true art of alchemy in his description of the fourteen stages. I hope with my little knowledge of the subject I have described just a few of the exciting things about the art of alchemy.

Final

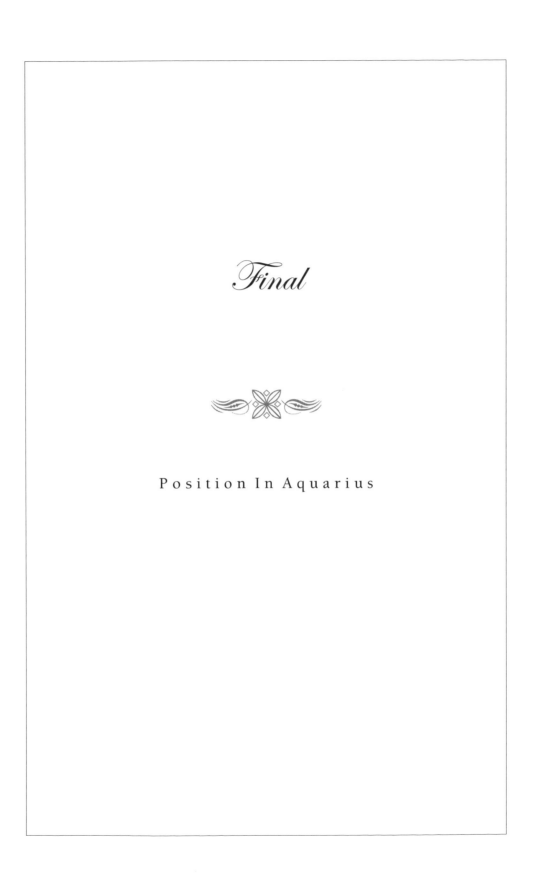

Position In Aquarius

~P o s i t i o n   I n   A q u a r i u s~

Priel:

Things we see…and things we don't see. Things we hear…and things we don't hear. What is really there? I know ultraviolet rays are there, but I don't see them. I know sound travels through wires, but I don't see it. I know oxygen is in the air, but I don't see it, hear it, taste it, smell it, or feel it. Yet, they are real, natural, and colossal. When I was a little girl sometimes I would hear a loud boom in the sky. I'd look up and nothing was there. But I knew what it was. One of the newly invented jet airplanes had flown over and broken the sound barrier. A native in the Amazons might have heard it and assumed it was an angry deity.

If I had told a modern person what I heard, who knew about jets, but not about their noisy boom when breaking the sound barrier, he might have told me that I only thought I heard something. Or, that it probably was thunder or a slamming door. That would have been something he knew existed.

Most definitely, things to wonder at really do happen. Some years back, for several weeks, at around 2:30 a.m., I had been waking up to hear a heavy weight press down on the wicker loveseat across from my bed. It sounded like all the straw crunching together under the weight of a person of about 175 pounds. The first time I thought it was a prowler, but no one was there. The following mornings I would describe it to my husband, a scientist and atheist, and he kept telling me that I must have heard a mouse. Then one night, again around 2:30 a.m., my husband, a heavy sleeper, raised cautiously straight up in bed and stared across at the wicker loveseat. He continued watching with puzzlement, then very slowly lay back down. The next morning I asked him why he had done that. He answered, "Probably it was nothing." On that particular night, I actually knew why he had raised up, because I had just heard that sound again and he obviously had heard it also. However, the next morning, he couldn't insist that it was a 175 POUND MOUSE! So he told me it was nothing. I tell this to make the point that people quite naturally deny what they don't understand.

What is paranormal, supernatural, metaphysical, or any other descriptive term one can give, might be just as natural as ultraviolet rays and oxygen. You said it earlier that it is all a natural part of the universe.

I could suggest that all the strange and inexplicable happenings which are so difficult to accept might be just the beginnings of what will be ordinary and understandable as we evolve, the same as the few geniuses in our world today will likely become the norm in times to come. It is fun to think about. However, throughout the subjects mentioned on all these pages, there has been a continuing thread from prior to creation until this time. It has been that there is an undeniable communication, presence, information, and influence in all things. That a universal presence surrounds us and is in us, resonating through all thought. That there is a master entity so vast that it reaches forever, and yet touches each one of us in the most gentle and intimate way.

When I look out at night and see the tiny lights in the dark sky, I think of early man gazing at them and wondering what such tiny lights could be. He couldn't see that one little light might be a galaxy made with billions and billions of those little lights. How much more is there that we only partially see? How long will it be before we see 'it all'? I wish I could be here!

When my daughter was six years old, she was watching admiringly as her eight year old brother read a book. She asked him, "Mickey, tell me about the world." My son paused a moment, then answered, "I can only tell you what I know."

Mr. Ashoorian, you very kindly agreed to tell some of what you know, based upon the things you read and studied. To the unexposed, some of the material can be surprising. And to some, the way you have expressed it, can be awakening. I've been fascinated with what you chose to share. Thank you, so much.

Ashoorian:

I really thank you. I truly couldn't have done it without you. You awakened me. I was wishing to say more about all the subjects, but as stated at the beginning, we were only to give the general idea about things. As you just remarked, there are people who will be shocked or skeptical about certain items. Well, those were not my ideas. Sages and masters for centuries have talked and written about them, and the results are what we see in books today. That is where we are in this, the twenty first, century. And now, I'd like to give my final thought.

We are in the Aquarian Age, in which remarkable changes are taking place. A very strong stream of spiritual vibration is penetrating human consciousness. We are recovering from that deep coma of the ages, and understand that the universe is a great intelligent mind, not a dead machine, and that human being is a spiritual soul. Once this is comprehended, there will be no fear of death, and we will understand that our soul is immortal.

A spiritual person is aware that human potentiality has no limits. He knows that behind all these disasters in our life, there is a divine power of transformation at work. That is what is happening in Aquarian Age. We have been told that during Aquarius the water of life will be poured down over all humanity. Many believe that the ever-coming one, the Christ, will come again in his newest guise in Aquarian Age. Edgar Cayce explained in one of his readings, "The cycle has rolled to that period when the individual entities again in the earth's experience gather together for a definite work."

We unconsciously are practicing the great work of alchemy to transform our life to a higher level of hierarchal stage and produce the real elixir or universal medicine for our salvation. But this cannot be accomplished without reaching to those high frequencies and tasting the bliss of spirituality.

I remember a few months before year 2000, people talked about the end of the world and desperately bought extra food, water, and so forth. I was confident that nothing would happen. I believed that, instead, a psychological transformation toward a great change will happen and transcend the mind of mankind to comprehend the higher level of spirituality.

Transformation into higher dimensions of spirituality will lead us deeper into the fifth round, or dimension, of mankind in which we will interact in an ethereal level like a world of radiance beyond our solid world.

As we talked earlier, spirituality cannot be learned and cannot be given to us. It should grow and happen within us. When this happens, the spiritual person will be aware of every moment of his life. He observes and respects all aspects of nature and his own human beings. It is said spiritual people breathe universal intelligence, and become their own messiah.

That is more than possible, because science says that human substances, or all that make up the body, are completely replaced every seven years. Therefore, we are not human 'being'…. we are human 'becoming'. We are becoming to be the master of the universe, and there is no limit for us to become our own messiah.

The world of today is so wild and dangerous to live in. Blood is shedding in each corner of the world. Pollution is killing our atmosphere. We are turning our living earth into a poisoning death planet. In such an unsecured world, in such a dazzling environment of our century, we must try to bring back with compassion the divine power to clean the killing poison of the atmosphere and sweep away all that is negative to create a new age which was prophesized for us in Aquarian Age. Otherwise, the Mother Nature will hit back intensely at us in a disastrous way as we have seen in the few last decades. We have to wake up and come out of this deadly coma! We have to learn how to save our planet and secure the future of our human race. This has been depicted in our destiny. The esoteric teaching tells us that in the fifth level of human life we will interact in a very high dimension and solve all of our physical problems. Buddhism tell us that the wheel of life spins and turns every 2,500 years, and now we are in the beginning of a new cycle in which we will act in a very high frequency as spiritual beings.

Yatri, the great spiritual master, in his book, *Unknown Man*, writes, "The first declaration of a new species of man is being born on Earth today. An extraordinary blueprint of mankind which reveals a rich and untouched endowment of miraculous talents which, once awakened, could lead us all to the natural state of mind."

This has happened, and will be happening more in the future. As I said earlier, human being will be the master of the universe, because it seems that this has been our heritage since the beginning of the human race. As Krishnamurti and Gurdjieff put it, in order to achieve that, there are some principles which would have the first priority in our life, like self knowledge, self observation, self remembering, and self development.

These principles will bring us out of ourselves and cross the distance between us and our creator…which is only one step. This will happen unconsciously. We have to keep in mind that unconsciousness is the most powerful divine essence in human life.

All these can be accomplished by unlimited power of the human mind. We can bring forth the new golden age of Aquarius which was prophesized for us by the great masters of the world. Many spiritual scientists believe that everything we encounter and experience through our senses in our meditative and contemplative state is composed of invisible tiny atoms and subatomic particles. When they come together there is a kind of form, but since they don't exist separately from space they have no genuinely solid existence. They can be energized by the power of the mind to be manifested in actual existence or dissolved to disappear completely.

This is the mastery of man in universe, and his position in which he will cross the boundaries of even more levels of his life and become one with his source. Man through meditation and contemplation will cure the wounds of the human soul and stop the blood shedding of innocent people. That would be the ultimate level of spirituality, the state of adoration, in which man will adore his creator.

End

Poems from Misha

A Symbolic Love Style for Antiquity

In Unfinished Dream

In the Absence of the Darkness

A Symbolic Love Style
for Antiquity

A Love For All Time

I was breathless in the deep silence of the void space,
You, like Brahma, the God of Creation,
    gave me your breath.

I was lost in an eternal darkness of life,
You, like Innana, the Goddess of love and compassion,
    nourished me and gave me motherly love.

I was a soul in an unmanifested dimension,
You, like Shiva, the God of recycling,
    manifested me in physical body to share my life with you!

I was wounded in soul and body, dwelled in the impurity of life,
You, like a Christ soul, poured the water of life over my body,
    and cleansed me from the impurity.

Oh! My very precious one, if I know you will be there for me,
I will wish to be reborn thousands of times,
    just to have you again.

MISHA ASHOORIAN

In Unfinished Dream

You and I, in an unfinished state of dreamlike, were born together,
to love beyond all the lovers.

We were born together, to taste the bliss of divine love
before creation.

You and I, were born together, to bring back the mythical love
of the ancients.

You and I, in that unfinished state of dream, were born together,
to sing the eternal melodies of the sphere.

We have, together, broken all the unlimited boundaries of
time and space, to learn how to love each other unconditionally.

My very precious one, you…just you alone, taught me how to
love and adore the Christ soul in my life.

MISHA ASHOORIAN

In the Absense of the Darkness

In the absence of the darkness,
is where I can take a free breath.

My target is beyond the sun,
and light is my eternal domain.

The legend of the fallen angels
is a forgotten legend,
Thus, the darkness cannot exist
when the light has taken over.

No tears are remained in my eyes,
to cry for the pain and sorrow of mankind.

I have embraced the absolute,
and etermal light of the Christ soul.

My precious one, come once again
for the last time,
to breathe together freely
in the absence of the darkness!

Come, to be together, the witnesses
of the second coming and resurrection of the Christ.

MISA ASHOORIAN

Notes

Notes

Notes